The Barbecue Cookbook

Oxmoor House®

Copyright 1988 by Oxmoor House, Inc.
Book Division of Southern Progress Corporation
P.O. Box 2463, Birmingham, Alabama 35201

Recipes adapted from *Southern Living*® cookbooks. *Southern Living*® is a federally registered trademark belonging to Southern Living, Inc.

Library of Congress Catalog Number: 88-060793

ISBN: 0-8487-0749-4

Manufactured in the United States of America
Second Printing 1989

THE BARBECUE COOKBOOK

Executive Editor: Ann H. Harvey
Senior Editor: Joan Erskine Denman
Assistant Foods Editor: Laura N. Massey
Copy Editor: Melinda E. West
Designer: Jane L. Bonds
Illustrator: Caroline Wellesley
Cover Photographer: Jim Bathie
Cover Stylist: Kay E. Clarke

Cover: *Picnic Barbecued Chicken* (page 35), *Mediterranean Spring Salad* (page 43), and *Corn-on-the-Cob with Herb Butter* (page 47).

Contents

Introduction

Barbecuing has come a long way since the days when the Spaniards arrived on the South Atlantic Coast to find the Indians cooking meat and fish on green wood racks over open fires or hot stones. This process was called boucan. The Spanish renamed it barbacoa, which eventually became barbecue. Later, the Colonials liked the smoked flavor so much that they made barbecuing a part of their social life. In the 1700's, the outdoor barbecue became the favorite gathering theme for New York society, while, at the same time, politicians adopted it as a rallying point for electioneering.

Over the years, barbecue has evolved regionally. From state to state, across the country, mopping and sopping sauces differ in color and intensity, ranging from tomato-red to transparent sneaky-hot. While the Deep South wants pork barbecue, Texas and Oklahoma prefer beef. In western Kentucky, mutton shares the honors with pork. Chicken emerges on top in eastern Tennessee, but pork is not far behind. If you travel far enough West, cabrito (goat meat) is the favorite.

COOKING METHODS

The term "barbecue" encompasses many different cooking methods, although basically it means to roast meat whole or in portions over an open fire or in a pit. Pit grilling, usually employed for a large affair, calls first for digging a pit about 3½ feet wide and deep. Next, the pit is filled with hot hardwood coals for fuel, then covered with sand or gravel, and topped with bundles of meat. Finally, the pit is covered with a sheet of iron supported by a steel pipe or rod.

Smoking is a process by which meat is cured by exposure to smoke. Since smoked meat looks different from meat cooked by other methods, color is not an accurate test for doneness, especially for pork and poultry. You should rely on a meat thermometer to determine the doneness of smoked meat.

Grilling is the action of cooking meat on a utensil of parallel bars. In this procedure, the meat is exposed to heat from charcoal or electricity, and the meat is moistened by marinating beforehand or basting during the grilling process.

Rotisserie cooking resembles the Indians' early methods of barbecuing. A spit is used to secure and rotate meat above a fire. If the piece of meat to be barbecued is large, it is important to use a meat thermometer in determining doneness. By placing a drip pan under the rotisserie rod and arranging coals around the pan, you can prevent flare-ups that can blacken or char the meat.

Oven and stove-top barbecuing are quick methods that call for baking or simmering meat in a barbecue sauce. These methods yield a very tender product with little or no effort.

TYPES OF GRILLS

Barbecue grills on today's market range from lightweight foldup braziers to permanently installed gas grills. They also vary in price. When buying a grill, consider these points: where you grill, how often you grill, what kind of food you cook, and the number of people you usually serve. Here are some specifics on the different types of grills to assist you in selecting the right one for your needs.

*Braziers: The basic model of this popular style has a shallow fire bowl supported with three or four legs. Additional features include half-hoods, covers, electric rotisseries, and wheels. Some braziers offer adjustable grids and draft doors for temperature control.

*Stationary Barbecue Fireplaces: Built in backyards or public picnic areas, these outdoor fireplaces are permanent structures made of brick or brick and fieldstone. They are excellent for barbecuing larger quantities of meat over an open fire.

*Cooking Kettles: Often described as large Dutch ovens on legs, these grills can be used for broiling or for cooking large cuts of meat by indirect heat with minimal attention. Year-round grilling, even on damp and windy days, is possible with cooking kettle grills. Some are designed with thermometers in the hood and some offer rotisserie attachments.

*Gas Grills: The main advantages of these year-round cooking units that are fueled with natural or bottled gas are quick starts and immediate heat control. If the grill is stationary, gas can be piped in from underground; if it is mobile, gas is provided in a portable tank. In some gas grills the gas is fed into burners under a bed of ceramic briquets or into infrared units in the lid of the grill. Many units are designed with an attached work surface.

*Hibachis: These Oriental-inspired grills vary greatly in size. They are usually made of cast iron and are most often used for hors d'oeuvres and small-scale barbecuing on a patio, porch, or even indoors.

*Electric Grills: The electric grill is another year-round cooking unit that requires no charcoal. It offers a range of temperature selection and improved heat control, which makes it unnecessary to raise or lower the grill grids. Rotisserie attachments are sometimes included.

THE PERFECT FIRE

Successful grilling starts with a good fire. The bed of coals should be prepared at least 30 minutes in advance of cooking. Stack charcoal briquets thickly in center of grill, about 8 coals deep; gradually slope down to 2 coals deep around edges.

To start a fire easily, use kindling and paper or an electric starter. If you use a chemical liquid starter, be sure it's odorless. Remember, once the fire is started, never add more liquid starter.

When the coals are coated with a fine layer of gray ash and are hot with no flames, use tongs to spread briquets quickly in a single layer and make a bed of coals large enough for the food that will be grilled. Be sure that the edges of the coals touch. For gas grills, double-check to see that the volcanic rock or briquets are in an even layer.

To test the temperature of the coals before adding the food, hold your hand at cooking height, palm-side down, above the coals. If you can leave your hand in position for 2 seconds, the coals are hot; 3 seconds, they are medium-hot; 4 seconds, they are medium, and 5 seconds, they are low. To lower the temperature, raise the grid(s) or spread the coals. To increase the temperature, lower the grid(s) and move coals closer together.

Once the charcoal is covered with ash, the fire will remain hot for 30 to 45 minutes, then the heat will gradually diminish. To keep heat constant for longer cooking times, add more charcoal briquets, a few at a time, along the outer edges. As long as edges of new coals are touching burning coals, they will ignite.

ENHANCING FLAVOR

Since grilling is a dry-heat method of cooking, lean cuts of meat, such as fish and poultry, can become tough and dry. You can avoid this by tenderizing the meat beforehand with a marinade containing wine, vinegar, pineapple juice, or another acidic liquid. Marinating improves the flavor and makes the meat tender and juicy. For the health-conscious cook, incorporating reduced-sodium soy sauce and herbs and spices

into a marinade mixture is a good way to reduce salt while still retaining flavor.

For flavor variety, baste meat with a marinade or sauce during all or part of the grilling process. If the basting sauce or marinade is high in sugar or other ingredients that burn easily, brush it on during the latter third of the cooking time.

While everyone knows cookouts are fun, dieters, especially, will benefit from barbecuing. When meat is cooked on a grill, excess fat drips onto the hot coals, leaving meat with fewer calories and a delicious smoky flavor. It is best, however, to select low-fat meats for grilling because too much fat dripping onto hot coals can create excess smoke and flare-ups that blacken or char meats.

The next time you use the grill, experiment with using wood smoke for seasoning your meat; most people are surprised and delighted by the distinctive flavors that result. Hickory wood is the old standby used for its strong dense-flavored smoke. Mesquite, oak, apple, and maple are fast becoming favorites, also. Basically, any hardwood will work well; however, never use wood from trees with needles, such as pine, fir, spruce, or cedar, since pitch from the wood adds an unpleasant taste to food.

Precut wood chips are available in grocery stores, but twigs or thin slices from fallen branches work just as well. You'll need to soak the wood in water at least 1 hour before adding it to the hot coals or heat source. Smoking wood is necessary so the wood will smolder and smoke rather than flame.

TIMELY TIPS

Barbecuing on the grill can be quick, especially if you use time-saving methods as you prepare. Save time and ensure success by gathering small grilling tools ahead of time on a large tray. Such tools include long-handled tongs, a timer, gloves or mitts, a spatula, a small long-handled cotton dishmop or brush for basting, and a water-mist bottle for extinguishing flare-ups. Carry this tray with you when you go to prepare your fire. When you bring the meat to the grill, make sure you also have the necessary seasonings and basting sauce or marinade. Running back to the kitchen at the last minute to grab a forgotten item may mean the difference between perfection and a charred disaster.

As you begin to grill your meat, follow these tips. First, remove the cooking grid(s) and spray them with vegetable cooking spray or grease them with shortening or vegetable oil. This is especially important when grilling fish. Fish is so lean and fragile that it will stick to an ungreased grid. For best results, select fish about 1 inch thick; thinner pieces tend to dry out or tear apart.

You may choose to purchase a wire grilling basket. It is ideal for supporting fish, meat patties, or steaks as they grill, and it simplifies the turning of your meat. Grease the wire basket lightly for best results.

Remember to keep a careful check on meat while it is grilling. Total cooking time will vary with the quality of charcoal, fire, and heat; cut of meat, and its position on the grill; the degree of doneness desired; and weather. To grill in cold or windy weather, increase cooking time and use more charcoal. If you use a covered grill, food will cook more quickly because there's less space to heat and the heat is confined and intense. When placing food on the grill leave space around each item to allow even cooking and smoke penetration. To prevent loss of flavorful juices, use tongs instead of a fork to handle meat.

Generally, grilling time for tenderloins, other roasts, and lean meat (such as chicken) is longer than for well-marbled steaks or other fatty meat. For large cuts of meat, it's best to use a meat thermometer to determine internal temperature and degree of doneness. Generally, the thinner the chops or steaks, the closer the grill grids should be to the coals. The thicker cuts should be grilled farther away from the coals in order to cook thoroughly.

Before cooking any chops or steaks, trim away excess fat to avoid flare-ups. Scoring the remaining fat on the outside edges will keep the meat from curling as it cooks.

Chicken has a tendency to burn on the grill, so cook it over medium-hot coals for best results. If the chicken begins to burn, place a disposable aluminum pan directly under the chicken to catch the drippings. Use tongs to push the hot coals around the sides of the pan.

Generally, fish is cooked 9 to 10 minutes per inch or until it flakes easily when tested with a fork. Basting fish frequently with a sauce, marinade, or melted butter during grilling helps to keep it moist.

Since its humble beginnings, barbecuing has evolved into a favorite pastime or hobby for many cooks. In a relaxed environment, the cook feels free to discover or create a variety of grilling techniques, many of which will be touted later as being the "only way to do it." Derived through much experimentation, barbecuing is an easily accomplished skill that provides edible results and lots of fun.

Beef

BARBECUED CHUCK ROAST

1 (3- to 4-pound) boneless chuck roast
   (2 to 3 inches thick)
4 cloves garlic, minced
¼ cup olive oil
1 teaspoon dried whole rosemary,
   crushed
2 teaspoons soy sauce
½ teaspoon dry mustard
¼ cup red wine vinegar
¼ cup sherry (optional)
2 tablespoons catsup
1½ teaspoons commercial steak sauce
½ teaspoon Worcestershire sauce

Place roast in a large shallow container. Sauté garlic in olive oil in a small skillet; add crushed rosemary, soy sauce, and dry mustard, stirring well. Remove from heat, and stir in red wine vinegar and sherry, if desired; pour over roast. Cover and refrigerate at least 8 hours, turning roast occasionally.

Remove roast from marinade, reserving marinade. Add catsup, steak sauce, and Worcestershire sauce to marinade, stirring well; baste roast with sauce. Insert meat thermometer into thickest part of roast, making sure it does not touch fat. Grill over hot coals 40 minutes or until thermometer registers 140° (rare), 160° (medium), or 170° (well done). Turn roast and baste frequently with sauce. Let stand 10 to 15 minutes before slicing. Yield: 6 to 8 servings.

SAUCY STOVE-TOP BARBECUE

1 (1½- to 2-pound) chuck roast
1 large onion, chopped
1 (10½-ounce) can consommé,
   undiluted
1 (8-ounce) can tomato sauce
1 cup catsup
¼ cup cider vinegar
¼ cup lemon juice
¼ cup chili sauce
¼ cup orange marmalade
2 tablespoons chopped fresh parsley
2 tablespoons frozen orange juice
   concentrate, thawed and undiluted
1 tablespoon Worcestershire sauce
2 teaspoons paprika
2 teaspoons chili powder
¼ teaspoon dried whole oregano
⅛ teaspoon garlic salt
Dash of hot sauce

Place roast in a Dutch oven; add water to cover roast, and bring to a boil. Cover, reduce heat, and simmer 1 hour. Uncover and cook over low heat an additional hour or until roast is tender. Drain off liquid. Remove and discard all fat and bone from roast; coarsely chop meat, and set aside.

Combine remaining ingredients in Dutch oven, stirring well; bring to a boil. Stir in meat. Reduce heat, and simmer, uncovered, 1 to 1½ hours, stirring occasionally. Yield: 6 servings.

BARBECUED RIB ROAST

2 tablespoons lemon-pepper seasoning, divided
1 (6- to 8-pound) boneless beef rib roast
Marinade (recipe follows)
Mesquite or oak chips
Savory Barbecue Sauce
Additional lemon-pepper seasoning

Rub 1 tablespoon lemon-pepper seasoning over surface of roast. Place roast in a large shallow container; pour marinade over roast. Cover and refrigerate 6 hours, turning roast occasionally.

Soak mesquite chips in water to cover for at least 1 hour. Drain and set aside.

Remove roast from marinade, reserving 2 cups marinade for use in Savory Barbecue Sauce. Rub remaining 1 tablespoon lemon-pepper seasoning over surface of roast. Insert meat thermometer into thickest part of roast, making sure it does not touch fat. Set roast aside.

Prepare fire in a covered grill; let burn until coals are gray. Rake coals to one end of grill; place wood chips over hot coals. Place roast at opposite end; cover with lid. Grill over indirect heat 2½ to 3 hours or until thermometer registers 140° (rare), 160° (medium), or 170° (well done). Baste every hour with Savory Barbecue Sauce. Sprinkle roast with additional lemon-pepper seasoning. Let stand 10 to 15 minutes before slicing. Serve with remaining sauce. Yield: 12 to 16 servings.

Marinade:

3½ cups water
1½ cups Burgundy or other dry red wine
¾ cup red wine vinegar
1 small onion, sliced
1 stalk celery, chopped
1 clove garlic, crushed

Combine all ingredients, stirring marinade well. Yield: 6 cups.

Savory Barbecue Sauce:

2 cups reserved marinade
2 cups beer
1 cup vegetable oil
¼ cup plus 2 tablespoons seasoning blend

Combine all ingredients, stirring sauce well. Yield: 5 cups.

DENTON, TEXAS, BARBECUED BEEF BRISKET

1 (4- to 6-pound) beef brisket
¾ cup red wine vinegar
½ cup firmly packed brown sugar
½ cup unsweetened pineapple juice
⅓ cup molasses
⅓ cup prepared mustard
1 tablespoon minced onion
3 tablespoons Worcestershire sauce
1 teaspoon chili powder
¼ teaspoon hot sauce

Place brisket in a zip-top heavy-duty plastic bag. Combine remaining ingredients, stirring well; pour over brisket, and secure bag tightly. Turn bag to coat brisket thoroughly. Place bag in a shallow container; refrigerate at least 4 hours, turning bag occasionally.

Remove brisket from marinade, reserving marinade. Prepare fire in a covered grill. Grill brisket over medium coals until browned. Cover with lid, and grill 15 minutes. Turn brisket, and baste with reserved marinade; set remaining marinade aside. Cover and grill brisket an additional 15 minutes.

Wrap brisket in heavy-duty aluminum foil, allowing room for marinade. Cut a hole in top of foil; pour remaining marinade through hole over brisket. Press foil together to seal hole. Cover and continue to grill over medium coals 1½ to 2 hours or until very tender. To serve, diagonally slice brisket across grain into thin slices. Yield: 12 to 16 servings.

GRILLED BRISKET WITH PANHANDLE BARBECUE SAUCE

1 (4- to 5-pound) beef brisket
1 tablespoon garlic salt
1½ teaspoons coarsely ground
   pepper
Panhandle Barbecue Sauce

Sprinkle brisket with garlic salt and pepper. Wrap brisket in heavy-duty aluminum foil. Prepare fire in a covered grill. Place brisket on grill. Cover with lid, and open vent. Grill over low coals 2 hours or until very tender.

To serve, diagonally slice brisket across grain into thin slices. Serve with Panhandle Barbecue Sauce. Yield: 12 servings.

Panhandle Barbecue Sauce:

2 (14-ounce) bottles catsup
1 cup firmly packed brown sugar
½ cup butter or margarine
3 tablespoons lemon juice
2 tablespoons liquid smoke
2 tablespoons Worcestershire
   sauce

Combine all ingredients in a large saucepan, stirring well; bring to a boil. Reduce heat, and simmer sauce, uncovered, 30 minutes, stirring occasionally. Yield: about 3½ cups.

TOURNEDOS DIABLES

1 (5- to 7-pound) beef tenderloin,
   trimmed
Garlic salt to taste
Coarsely ground pepper to taste
1 (6-ounce) package long grain and
   wild rice
2 cups beef bouillon
⅓ cup sherry
¼ cup cognac
2 teaspoons butter or margarine
1 tablespoon plus 1 teaspoon Dijon
   mustard
1 tablespoon tomato paste
1 teaspoon Worcestershire sauce
½ teaspoon garlic powder
½ teaspoon vinegar
1 cup sliced fresh mushrooms
1 cup chopped green onions

Sprinkle tenderloin with garlic salt and pepper. Insert meat thermometer into tenderloin, making sure it does not touch fat. Grill over medium coals 15 minutes on each side or until thermometer registers 140° (rare), 160° (medium), or 170° (well done). Set aside, and keep warm.

Prepare rice according to package directions. Set aside, and keep warm.

Place bouillon in a medium saucepan, and bring to a boil. Reduce heat, and simmer bouillon, uncovered, while completing recipe.

Combine sherry and cognac in a small, long-handled saucepan; heat just until warm (do not boil). Remove from heat. Immediately ignite sherry mixture with a long match, and pour over bouillon. When flames die down, stir in butter, Dijon mustard, tomato paste, Worcestershire sauce, ½ teaspoon garlic powder, and vinegar. Cook, uncovered, over low heat 15 minutes. Stir in mushrooms and green onions; cook an additional 5 minutes. Remove sauce from heat.

Cut tenderloin into ½-inch slices. Place rice on a serving platter; top with meat and sauce. Yield: 8 to 10 servings.

MARINATED BARBECUED CHUCK STEAK

1 (2-pound) chuck steak (about 1 inch thick)
⅓ cup lemon juice
¼ cup olive oil
2 tablespoons minced onion
1 clove garlic, minced
1 tablespoon chili powder
1 teaspoon salt
2 teaspoons ground ginger

Trim excess fat from steak, and place steak in a large shallow container. Combine remaining ingredients, stirring well; pour marinade over steak. Cover and marinate in refrigerator at least 8 hours, turning steak once.

Remove steak from marinade. Grill over hot coals 8 to 10 minutes on each side or until desired degree of doneness. Yield: 2 servings.

SAUCY OVEN-BARBECUED STEAK

2 pounds boneless round steak
1 tablespoon vegetable oil
¾ cup catsup
½ cup water
½ cup cider vinegar
1 tablespoon brown sugar
1 tablespoon prepared mustard
1 tablespoon Worcestershire sauce
½ teaspoon salt
⅛ teaspoon pepper

Trim excess fat from round steak, and cut steak into serving-size pieces. Heat 1 tablespoon vegetable oil in a large heavy skillet; add steak, and brown evenly on both sides. Transfer steak to a 2-quart shallow baking dish.

Combine remaining ingredients, stirring well; pour over steak. Cover and bake at 325° for 1½ hours or until tender. Yield: 6 to 8 servings.

GRILLED BLACK PEPPER STEAK

2 (1½- to 2-pound) sirloin steaks (1½ to 2 inches thick)
2 large onions, thinly sliced
2 cloves garlic, minced
2 cups red wine vinegar
1 cup vegetable oil
⅔ cup firmly packed brown sugar
½ teaspoon salt
½ teaspoon dried whole marjoram
½ teaspoon dried whole rosemary, crushed
6 drops of hot sauce
2 tablespoons plus 2 teaspoons coarsely ground pepper, divided

Trim excess fat from steaks, and place steaks in a large shallow container. Combine remaining ingredients except pepper, stirring well; pour over steaks. Cover and refrigerate 3 hours, turning steaks occasionally.

Remove steaks from marinade. Press 2 teaspoons pepper into each side of each steak. Grill steaks over hot coals 15 minutes on each side or until desired degree of doneness. Yield: 6 servings.

TANGY FLANK STEAK

1 (1- to 1½-pound) flank steak
½ cup vegetable oil
1 tablespoon plus 1½ teaspoons chopped fresh parsley
3 tablespoons vinegar
3 tablespoons lemon juice
2 tablespoons Worcestershire sauce
2 tablespoons soy sauce
1½ teaspoons salt
2 teaspoons dry mustard
1 teaspoon freshly ground pepper
½ teaspoon garlic salt

Place steak in a large shallow container. Combine remaining ingredients, stirring well; pour over steak. Cover and refrigerate 2 hours, turning steak frequently.

Remove steak from marinade. Grill over hot coals 10 to 12 minutes on each side or until desired degree of doneness. To serve, diagonally slice steak across grain into thin slices. Yield: 4 to 6 servings.

FLANK STEAK PINWHEELS

2 (1- to 1½-pound) flank steaks
2 cups chopped onion
4 cloves garlic, minced
1 cup vegetable oil
⅔ cup vinegar
2 teaspoons salt
½ teaspoon dried whole thyme
½ teaspoon dried whole marjoram
Dash of pepper

Diagonally slice steaks across grain into ¼-inch-thick slices; roll up slices, and secure with wooden picks. Place pinwheels in a 13- x 9- x 2-inch baking dish; sprinkle with chopped onion. Combine remaining ingredients, stirring well; pour marinade over pinwheels. Cover and refrigerate at least 8 hours.

Remove pinwheels from marinade. Grill over medium-hot coals 14 to 16 minutes or until desired degree of doneness, turning pinwheels frequently. Yield: 8 to 10 servings.

FAVORITE FAJITAS

1 pound flank or skirt steak
Juice of 2 to 3 limes
1 to 1½ teaspoons garlic salt
½ teaspoon pepper
4 (8-inch) flour tortillas
Vegetable toppings or sauce (optional)

Place steak in a zip-top heavy-duty plastic bag. Combine juice, garlic salt, and pepper, stirring well; pour over steak, and secure bag tightly. Turn bag to coat steak thoroughly. Place bag in a large shallow container; refrigerate 6 to 8 hours, turning bag occasionally.

Wrap tortillas in aluminum foil, and bake at 325° for 15 minutes or until thoroughly heated. Set tortillas aside, and keep warm.

Remove steak from marinade. Grill over medium-hot mesquite coals 5 to 6 minutes on each side or until desired degree of doneness.

Diagonally slice steak across grain into thin slices. Wrap tortillas around steak, and top with any of the following ingredients, if desired: chopped tomato, green onions, guacamole, sour cream, picante sauce, or taco sauce. Yield: 4 servings.

BARBECUED BEEF SHORT RIBS

1 tablespoon butter or margarine
⅓ cup chopped onion
1 tablespoon plus 1 teaspoon all-purpose flour
1 cup apple cider or apple juice
3 tablespoons sweet pickle relish
1 tablespoon catsup
¼ teaspoon salt
¼ teaspoon dried whole basil
⅛ teaspoon ground allspice
Dash of ground cloves
4 pounds beef short ribs

Melt butter in a medium saucepan over low heat; add chopped onion, and sauté until onion is tender. Add flour, stirring well. Cook 1 minute, stirring constantly. Gradually add apple cider, and cook over medium heat, stirring constantly, until mixture thickens. Stir in remaining ingredients except ribs. Remove sauce from heat, and set aside.

Cut ribs into serving-size pieces, and grill over low coals 1 hour and 10 minutes. Baste ribs with sauce, and grill an additional 20 minutes or until desired degree of doneness. Turn and baste frequently with sauce. Serve ribs with remaining sauce. Yield: 4 servings.

OVEN-BARBECUED BEEF SHORT RIBS

3 pounds beef short ribs
1 cup catsup
¾ cup firmly packed brown sugar
½ cup chopped onion
1 clove garlic, minced
½ cup water
½ cup vinegar
1 (6-ounce) can tomato paste
2 tablespoons prepared mustard
2 teaspoons salt

Cut ribs into serving-size pieces, and brown evenly on all sides in a large heavy skillet (do not add oil or shortening). Cover and cook over low heat 1 hour. Drain off pan drippings.

Combine remaining ingredients, stirring well; pour over ribs in skillet. Cover and continue to cook over low heat 1½ hours or until meat is tender. Yield: about 4 servings.

PINEAPPLE-BEEF KABOBS

3 pounds boneless sirloin tip roast, cut into 1½-inch cubes
2 (20-ounce) cans pineapple chunks, undrained
⅔ cup cider vinegar
⅔ cup catsup
½ cup firmly packed brown sugar
¼ cup soy sauce
2 teaspoons ground ginger
1½ teaspoons liquid smoke
½ pound fresh mushroom caps
2 small onions, quartered
2 medium-size green peppers, cut into 1-inch pieces

Place meat cubes in a large shallow container. Drain pineapple, reserving juice. Set pineapple chunks aside. Combine pineapple juice and next 6 ingredients, stirring well; pour over meat. Cover and refrigerate at least 8 hours, stirring meat occasionally.

Remove meat from marinade. Pour marinade into a medium saucepan; bring to a boil, and add mushroom caps. Reduce heat, and simmer, uncovered, 10 minutes. Drain, reserving marinade. Set mushroom caps aside.

Alternate meat, pineapple, mushrooms, onion, and green pepper on skewers. Grill kabobs over medium-hot coals 15 minutes or until desired degree of doneness. Turn and baste frequently with marinade. Yield: 8 to 10 servings.

BEEF KABOBS DELUXE

2 pounds boneless sirloin tip roast, cut into 2-inch cubes
½ cup vegetable oil
¼ cup soy sauce
¼ cup vinegar
½ teaspoon pepper
6 to 8 boiling onions
½ pound fresh mushrooms
1 cup cherry tomatoes
1 large green pepper, cut into 1-inch pieces

Place meat cubes in a large shallow container. Combine oil, soy sauce, vinegar, and pepper, stirring well; pour over meat. Cover and refrigerate at least 4 hours, stirring meat occasionally.

Parboil onions 3 to 5 minutes. Drain. Remove meat from marinade, reserving marinade. Alternate meat and vegetables on skewers. Grill kabobs over medium coals 5 minutes on each side or until desired degree of doneness. Baste frequently with marinade. Yield: 6 to 8 servings.

SKEWERED STEAK WITH VEGETABLES

2 pounds boneless sirloin steak
½ cup Chablis or other dry white wine
½ cup vegetable oil
2 tablespoons chili sauce
1 tablespoon vinegar
1 teaspoon Worcestershire sauce
½ teaspoon salt
½ teaspoon dried whole oregano
½ teaspoon dried whole thyme
1 clove garlic, crushed
½ pound fresh mushroom caps
2 large green peppers, cut into 1½-inch pieces
1 pint cherry tomatoes
4 small yellow squash, cut into 1-inch-thick slices

Trim excess fat from steak, and cut steak into 1-inch cubes. Place meat cubes in a large shallow container. Combine wine and next 8 ingredients, stirring well; pour over meat. Cover and refrigerate at least 2 hours, stirring meat occasionally.

Remove meat from marinade, reserving marinade. Alternate meat and vegetables on skewers. Grill kabobs over medium coals 15 minutes or until desired degree of doneness. Turn and baste frequently with marinade. Yield: 6 to 8 servings.

MARINATED BEEF KABOBS

1 pound boneless sirloin steak
1 (8-ounce) bottle Russian salad dressing
2 tablespoons lemon juice
1 tablespoon Worcestershire sauce
⅛ teaspoon garlic powder
⅛ teaspoon pepper
About 10 slices bacon, cut in half
2 medium-size green peppers, cut into 1-inch pieces
1 large onion, cut into 2-inch pieces
½ pound fresh mushrooms
1 pint cherry tomatoes

Trim excess fat from steak; cut into 1½-inch cubes. Place meat cubes in a shallow container. Combine dressing and next 4 ingredients, stirring well; pour over meat. Cover and refrigerate at least 8 hours, stirring meat occasionally.

Remove meat from marinade, reserving marinade. Wrap bacon around meat cubes; secure with wooden picks. Alternate meat and vegetables on skewers. Grill kabobs over medium-hot coals 10 minutes or until desired degree of doneness. Turn and baste frequently with marinade. Yield: 4 servings.

POOR BOY FILLETS

1 pound ground beef
1 (4-ounce) can mushroom stems and pieces, drained
¼ cup grated Parmesan cheese
3 tablespoons finely chopped pimiento-stuffed olives
2 tablespoons finely chopped green pepper
2 tablespoons finely chopped onion
½ teaspoon salt
½ teaspoon lemon-pepper seasoning
6 slices bacon

Shape ground beef into a 12- x 7½-inch rectangle on wax paper. Combine remaining ingredients except bacon, stirring well; sprinkle evenly over beef.

Starting at short end, roll up jellyroll fashion, lifting wax paper to support ground beef while rolling. Carefully slide beef roll onto a baking sheet, seam side down. Smooth and shape beef roll, using your hands. Cover and refrigerate roll 2 to 3 hours.

Cook bacon until limp but not brown. Drain. Cut beef roll into 1½-inch-thick slices. Wrap a slice of bacon around edge of each fillet; secure with wooden picks. Grill fillets over hot coals 8 minutes on each side or until desired degree of doneness. Yield: 6 servings.

SEASONED BURGERS

1 pound ground chuck
2 tablespoons chopped green pepper
1 tablespoon dried onion flakes
1 tablespoon prepared horseradish
2 teaspoons Worcestershire sauce
2 teaspoons prepared mustard
½ teaspoon chili powder
¼ teaspoon salt
⅛ teaspoon pepper
Lettuce leaves
4 hamburger buns
4 slices process American cheese

Combine first 9 ingredients, stirring until combined. Shape mixture into 4 patties. Grill over medium coals 4 to 5 minutes on each side or until desired degree of doneness. Place lettuce on bottom half of each bun; top with a meat patty and cheese slice. Cover with top of bun, and serve. Yield: 4 servings.

STUFFED HAMBURGERS

2 tablespoons butter or margarine
1¼ cups herb-seasoned stuffing mix
1 (4-ounce) can chopped mushrooms, drained
1 egg, beaten
⅓ cup beef broth
¼ cup sliced green onions
¼ cup chopped almonds, toasted
1 teaspoon lemon juice
3 pounds ground beef
1 teaspoon salt
Lettuce leaves
8 hamburger buns
8 slices process American cheese

Melt butter in a medium saucepan over low heat; remove from heat. Stir in stuffing mix and next 6 ingredients. Set stuffing mixture aside.

Combine ground beef and salt, stirring until combined. Shape into 16 patties. Top 8 patties with ¼ cup stuffing mixture on each. Cover with remaining patties, pinching edges together to seal. Place patties in a lightly greased wire grilling basket. Grill over medium coals 10 to 12 minutes on each side or until desired degree of doneness. Place lettuce on bottom half of each bun; top with a meat patty and cheese slice. Cover with top of bun, and serve. Yield: 8 servings.

FRANKFURTERS WITH CONDIMENTS

12 beef frankfurters
12 frankfurter buns
Prepared mustard
Mayonnaise
Catsup
1 cup sweet pickle relish
1 medium onion, chopped
1 (8-ounce) package sharp Cheddar cheese, shredded
1 (15½-ounce) can chili without beans (optional)

Grill frankfurters over hot coals, turning frequently, until browned.

Spread cut sides of buns with desired amounts of mustard, mayonnaise, and catsup. Add frankfurters; top with pickle relish, onion, and cheese. Heat chili thoroughly, and spoon over frankfurters, if desired. Yield: 12 servings.

Fish & Shellfish

GRILLED STRIPED BASS

6 (¾-inch-thick) striped bass steaks
  (about 2 pounds)
½ cup butter or margarine, melted
⅓ cup sherry
⅓ cup lemon juice
1 clove garlic, minced
3 tablespoons soy sauce
2 tablespoons dillweed
1 teaspoon salt
2 tablespoons butter, melted

Rinse fish thoroughly in cold water; pat dry, and place in a large shallow container. Combine ½ cup melted butter and next 6 ingredients, stirring well; pour over fish. Cover and refrigerate 30 minutes, turning fish once.

Remove fish from marinade, reserving marinade. Grill over hot coals 10 minutes on each side or until fish flakes easily when tested with a fork. Baste frequently with marinade. Transfer to a serving platter, and pour 2 tablespoons melted butter evenly over fish. Yield: 6 servings.

BARBECUED BASS

8 (¼-pound) freshwater bass fillets
1 teaspoon salt
¼ teaspoon pepper
¼ teaspoon paprika
8 slices bacon, divided
1 tablespoon plus 1 teaspoon lemon
  juice, divided

Rinse fillets thoroughly in cold water; pat dry, and sprinkle with salt, pepper, and paprika. Set fillets aside.

Place 2 slices bacon on a large piece of heavy-duty aluminum foil; place a bass fillet lengthwise on each bacon slice. Sprinkle ½ teaspoon lemon juice over each fillet. Fold foil edges over, and wrap securely. Repeat procedure with remaining ingredients to make 3 additional packets.

Grill packets over hot coals 10 minutes. Turn packets, and grill an additional 10 minutes or until fish flakes easily when tested with a fork. Yield: 4 servings.

GRILLED SESAME CATFISH

½ cup vegetable oil
½ cup sesame seeds
¼ cup lemon juice
1 teaspoon salt
Dash of pepper
6 (⅔-pound) dressed catfish

Combine all ingredients except catfish, stirring well. Set lemon juice mixture aside.

Rinse fish thoroughly in cold water; pat dry, and place in a well-greased wire grilling basket. Grill over medium coals 12 minutes on each side or until fish flakes easily when tested with a fork. Baste catfish frequently with lemon juice mixture. Yield: 6 servings.

GRILLED BLUEFISH

6 (½-pound) bluefish fillets
1 cup commercial barbecue sauce or
**   see Sauce chapter**

Rinse fillets thoroughly in cold water; pat dry, and place in a lightly greased wire grilling basket. Grill over hot coals 3 to 5 minutes on each side or until fish flakes easily when tested with a fork. Baste frequently with sauce. Yield: 6 servings.

GRILLED KING MACKEREL

1½ pounds king mackerel fillets
8 slices white bread
¼ cup plus 2 tablespoons butter or
**   margarine, softened**
2 tablespoons lemon juice

Rinse fillets thoroughly in cold water; pat dry. Grill over hot coals 10 minutes on each side or until fish flakes easily when tested with a fork. Remove from grill, and keep warm.

Lightly toast bread slices on both sides. Combine softened butter and lemon juice; beat at medium speed of an electric mixer until smooth. Spread over hot toast; cut toast in half, and top with fish. Yield: 4 servings.

GRILLED GROUPER

½ cup olive oil
1 tablespoon plus 1½ teaspoons grated
**   Parmesan cheese**
1 tablespoon minced onion
2 teaspoons salt
¾ teaspoon sugar
¾ teaspoon dry mustard
¾ teaspoon pepper
¾ teaspoon dried whole basil
¾ teaspoon dried whole oregano
¼ cup red wine vinegar
1 tablespoon lemon juice
1 (2-pound) grouper fillet

Combine first 9 ingredients in container of an electric blender; cover and process 30 seconds. Add vinegar and lemon juice; process an additional 30 seconds. Set olive oil mixture aside.

Rinse fillet thoroughly in cold water; pat dry. Place in a lightly greased wire grilling basket. Grill over hot coals 10 minutes on each side or until fish flakes easily when tested with a fork. Baste frequently with olive oil mixture. Yield: 6 servings.

LEMON-GRILLED ORANGE ROUGHY

4 (¼-pound) orange roughy fillets
1 tablespoon butter or margarine,
**   melted**
½ teaspoon dried whole thyme
½ teaspoon grated lemon rind
2 tablespoons lemon juice
¼ teaspoon salt
¼ teaspoon paprika
Dash of garlic powder

Rinse fillets thoroughly in cold water; pat dry. Combine remaining ingredients, stirring well; baste fillets with lemon mixture. Grill over hot coals 5 minutes on each side or until fish flakes easily when tested with a fork. Yield: 4 servings.

MARINATED GRILLED TROUT

6 (¾-pound) dressed freshwater trout,
**   butterflied**
Marinade (recipe follows)
1 tablespoon chopped fresh chives
6 fresh thyme sprigs
6 lemon wedges

Rinse fish thoroughly in cold water; pat dry, and place in a large shallow container. Pour marinade over fish. Cover and refrigerate 4 hours, turning fish once.

Remove fish from marinade, reserving marinade. Open butterflied fillets, and place skin side down on grill. Sprinkle with chives, and top each fillet with a sprig of thyme. Lightly squeeze juice from lemon wedges over fish; place one lemon wedge on top of each fillet. Grill butterflied fillets over medium coals 10 minutes or until fish flakes easily when tested with a fork. Baste frequently with marinade. Yield: 6 servings.

Marinade:

1 cup vegetable oil
1 tablespoon plus 1 teaspoon salt
2 tablespoons grated Parmesan cheese
1½ teaspoons sugar
1½ teaspoons Worcestershire sauce
½ cup vinegar
2 tablespoons lemon juice

Combine first 5 ingredients in container of an electric blender; cover and process 30 seconds. Add vinegar and lemon juice; process an additional 30 seconds. Cover and refrigerate marinade until ready to use. Yield: about 1½ cups.

CEDARVALE GARDENS TROUT IDA

6 (¾-pound) dressed freshwater trout, butterflied
1 (16-ounce) bottle commercial Italian salad dressing

Rinse fish thoroughly in cold water; pat dry, and place in a large shallow container. Pour dressing over fish. Cover and refrigerate 4 hours, turning fish once.

Remove fish from marinade. Grill skin side down over hot coals 10 minutes or until fish flakes easily when tested with a fork. Yield: 6 servings.

GRILLED SHARK

6 (½-inch-thick) shark steaks (1½ pounds)
¼ cup plus 2 tablespoons commercial Italian salad dressing
¼ cup water
1½ teaspoons dried whole basil
1½ teaspoons chopped fresh parsley
1½ teaspoons lemon juice
1½ teaspoons dry sherry
⅛ teaspoon garlic powder

Rinse fish thoroughly in cold water; pat dry. Combine remaining ingredients, stirring well; baste fish with dressing mixture. Set remaining mixture aside.

Place fish in a well-greased wire grilling basket. Grill over medium coals 6 to 8 minutes on each side or until fish flakes easily when tested with a fork. Baste frequently with remaining dressing mixture. Yield: 6 servings.

GRILLED SWORDFISH

6 (1-inch-thick) swordfish steaks (about 2 pounds)
½ cup vegetable oil
¼ cup lemon juice
2 teaspoons salt
½ teaspoon Worcestershire sauce
¼ teaspoon white pepper
Dash of hot sauce
⅛ teaspoon paprika, divided

Rinse fish thoroughly in cold water; pat dry. Combine remaining ingredients except paprika, stirring well; baste fish with lemon juice mixture, and sprinkle with half of paprika. Set remaining lemon juice mixture and paprika aside.

Place fish in a well-greased wire grilling basket. Grill over medium coals 8 minutes on each side or until fish flakes easily when tested with a fork. Baste frequently with remaining lemon juice mixture, and sprinkle with remaining paprika. Yield: 6 servings.

GRILLED TUNA STEAKS

12 (1-inch-thick) tuna steaks (about 6
   pounds)
1 cup lemon juice
½ cup soy sauce
2 bay leaves
½ teaspoon dried whole thyme

Rinse fish thoroughly in cold water; pat
dry, and place in a large shallow container. Combine remaining ingredients,
stirring well; pour over fish. Cover and
refrigerate 1 hour, turning fish frequently.

Remove fish from marinade, reserving
marinade. Place fish in 2 well-greased
wire grilling baskets. Grill over hot coals
20 minutes or until fish flakes easily when
tested with a fork. Turn and baste occasionally with marinade. Yield: 12 servings.

GRILLED SALMON STEAKS

½ cup butter or margarine, melted
Juice of 1 lemon
½ teaspoon salt
¼ teaspoon white pepper
4 (1-inch-thick) salmon steaks (about
   1½ pounds)
1½ teaspoons chopped fresh dillweed

Combine first 4 ingredients, stirring
well. Set butter mixture aside.

Rinse fish thoroughly in cold water; pat
dry, and place in a lightly greased wire
grilling basket. Grill over medium coals 10
minutes on each side or until fish flakes
easily when tested with a fork. Baste frequently with half of butter mixture. Add
dillweed to remaining butter mixture, stirring well. Serve fish with dill-butter sauce.
Yield: 4 servings.

BARBECUED MARLIN

4 pounds white marlin, cut into 1-inch
   cubes
½ cup Worcestershire sauce
½ cup teriyaki sauce
½ cup lemon juice
½ cup butter or margarine, melted
2 teaspoons curry powder
1 teaspoon pepper

Place fish cubes in a large shallow container. Combine remaining ingredients,
stirring well; pour over fish. Cover and
marinate in refrigerator 1 hour, stirring
fish occasionally.

Remove fish from marinade, reserving
marinade. Thread fish on skewers. Grill
skewered fish over medium coals 5 minutes on each side or until fish flakes easily
when tested with a fork. Baste frequently
with marinade. Transfer fish to a serving
platter. Serve fish on wooden picks.
Yield: 24 appetizer servings.

SCALLOP-BACON KABOBS

1 pound fresh or frozen scallops,
   thawed
1 small pineapple, cut into 1-inch
   pieces
18 fresh mushroom caps
3 medium-size green peppers, cut into
   1-inch pieces
18 cherry tomatoes
¼ cup vegetable oil
¼ cup lemon juice
¼ cup Chablis or other dry white wine
¼ cup soy sauce
2 tablespoons chopped fresh parsley
½ teaspoon salt
½ teaspoon pepper
¼ teaspoon garlic powder
12 slices bacon, cut in half

Place scallops, pineapple pieces, and
vegetables in a large shallow container.
Combine remaining ingredients except
bacon, stirring well; pour over mixture in

container. Cover and refrigerate 1 to 1½ hours, stirring frequently.

Cook bacon until limp but not brown. Drain and set aside.

Remove scallops, pineapple, and vegetables from marinade, reserving marinade. Alternate with bacon on skewers. Grill kabobs over hot coals 10 to 12 minutes or until bacon is crisp. Turn and baste frequently with marinade. Yield: 6 servings.

GROUPER KABOBS

1 (16-ounce) can pineapple chunks, undrained
2 pounds grouper fillets, cut into 1-inch cubes
2 medium-size green peppers, cut into 1-inch pieces
½ cup soy sauce
¼ cup sherry
2 tablespoons brown sugar
1 teaspoon ground ginger
1 teaspoon dry mustard
1 clove garlic, minced

Drain pineapple, reserving ¼ cup juice. Alternate pineapple chunks, fish, and green pepper on skewers. Place kabobs in a large shallow container. Set aside.

Combine reserved juice, soy sauce, sherry, sugar, ginger, mustard, and garlic, stirring well; pour over kabobs. Cover and refrigerate at least 1 hour, turning kabobs occasionally.

Remove kabobs from marinade, reserving marinade. Grill kabobs over medium-hot coals 15 minutes or until fish flakes easily when tested with a fork. Turn and baste frequently with marinade. Yield: 6 servings.

PARTY BARBECUED SHRIMP

2 pounds large fresh shrimp, unpeeled
½ cup vegetable oil
½ cup lemon juice
¼ cup soy sauce
3 tablespoons finely chopped parsley
2 tablespoons finely chopped onion
1 clove garlic, crushed
½ teaspoon salt
½ teaspoon pepper

Peel and devein shrimp, and place in a large shallow container. Combine remaining ingredients, stirring well; pour over shrimp. Cover and refrigerate 2 to 3 hours, stirring shrimp occasionally.

Remove shrimp from marinade, and thread on skewers. Grill skewered shrimp over medium coals 3 to 4 minutes on each side or until desired degree of doneness. Transfer shrimp to a serving platter. Serve shrimp on wooden picks. Yield: 12 appetizer servings.

MARINATED AND GRILLED SHRIMP

2 pounds large fresh shrimp, unpeeled
⅓ cup sherry
⅓ cup sesame seed oil
⅓ cup soy sauce
½ teaspoon sugar
¼ teaspoon garlic powder
¼ teaspoon ground ginger

Peel and devein shrimp, and place in a large shallow container. Combine remaining ingredients, stirring well; pour over shrimp. Cover and refrigerate 2 to 3 hours, stirring shrimp occasionally.

Remove shrimp from marinade, reserving marinade. Thread shrimp on skewers. Grill over medium-hot coals 3 to 4 minutes on each side or until desired degree of doneness. Baste frequently with marinade. Yield: 6 servings.

GRILLED LOBSTER TAILS

¼ **cup plus 2 tablespoons butter,
    melted**
2 **tablespoons lemon juice**
½ **teaspoon salt**
⅛ **teaspoon pepper**
⅛ **teaspoon dried whole tarragon**
6 **frozen lobster tails, thawed**

Combine all ingredients except lobster
tails, stirring well. Set sauce aside.

Split lobster tails lengthwise, cutting
through upper shell and meat to, but not
through, bottom shell. Press shell halves
apart to expose meat; baste with sauce.
Set remaining sauce aside.

Place lobster tails, shell side down, on
grill. Grill over medium coals 20 minutes.
Turn lobster, and grill an additional 5 min-
utes or until desired degree of doneness.
Serve lobster with remaining sauce.
Yield: 6 servings.

SMOKEHOUSE OYSTERS

Hickory chips
Rock salt
1 **dozen oysters on the half shell,
    drained**
⅛ **teaspoon salt**
⅛ **teaspoon pepper**
¼ **cup butter or margarine, softened**
2 **tablespoons finely chopped green
    onions**
2 **tablespoons finely chopped fresh
    parsley**
3 **tablespoons cornflake crumbs**
3 **tablespoons grated Parmesan cheese**

Soak hickory chips in water to cover for
at least 1 hour. Drain and set aside.

Sprinkle a thin layer of rock salt in a 13-
x 9- x 2-inch baking pan lined with heavy-
duty aluminum foil. Arrange oysters (in
shells) over rock salt; sprinkle oysters
with salt and pepper. Combine softened
butter, green onions, and parsley, stirring
well; dot each oyster with butter mixture.
Combine remaining ingredients, stirring
well; sprinkle over butter mixture. Set
oysters aside.

Prepare fire in a covered grill; let burn
until coals are gray. Place wood chips
over hot coals. Place pan of oysters on
grill, and cover grill with lid. Grill over
gray coals 20 minutes or until crumbs are
browned and oyster edges curl. Yield: 4
appetizer servings.

NOTE: Rock salt is used to hold shells
upright and keep oysters hot.

GRILLED SOFT-SHELL CRABS

1 **cup vegetable oil**
2 **tablespoons vinegar**
1 **teaspoon salt**
1 **teaspoon lemon-pepper seasoning**
1 **teaspoon lemon juice**
¼ **teaspoon dried whole tarragon**
⅛ **teaspoon garlic powder**
12 **dressed soft-shell crabs**

Combine all ingredients except crabs,
stirring until blended. Cover and refrigerate sauce at least 8 hours.

Position crabs securely, back side
down, in a wire grilling basket. Grill over
hot coals 10 minutes, basting frequently
with sauce. Turn crabs, and grill an additional 5 minutes or until desired degree of
doneness. Baste frequently with remaining sauce. Yield: 6 servings.

Lamb

OVEN-BARBECUED LAMB

1 (8½- to 9-pound) leg of lamb
1 clove garlic, sliced
⅔ cup all-purpose flour
1 teaspoon salt
1 teaspoon ground ginger
1 teaspoon dry mustard
½ teaspoon pepper
2 tablespoons chili sauce
2 tablespoons olive oil
1 tablespoon Worcestershire sauce
1 tablespoon vinegar
2 medium onions, sliced
1 cup boiling water

Trim excess fat from leg of lamb. Using a sharp knife, cut several small slits on outside of lamb; stuff with garlic slices. Combine flour, salt, ginger, mustard, and pepper, stirring well; rub over surface of lamb. Set lamb aside.

Combine chili sauce, oil, Worcestershire sauce, and vinegar, stirring until blended. Set sauce aside.

Place lamb, fat side up, in a shallow roasting pan. Insert meat thermometer into lamb, making sure it does not touch bone or fat. Arrange onion slices around lamb. Baste with sauce.

Bake, uncovered, at 400° for 25 minutes. Reduce heat to 350°, and bake an additional hour and 15 minutes or until thermometer registers 140° (rare) or 160° (medium). Baste lamb every 15 minutes with sauce. Add boiling water to pan during last hour of baking time.

Transfer lamb and onion slices to a serving platter, discarding pan drippings. Let stand 10 minutes before slicing. Serve lamb with remaining sauce. Yield: about 12 servings.

GRILLED LEG OF LAMB

Hickory chips
1 (7- to 8-pound) leg of lamb
15 cloves garlic, sliced
1 teaspoon salt
½ teaspoon pepper
½ teaspoon dried whole
   oregano

Soak hickory chips in water to cover for at least 1 hour. Drain and set aside.

Trim excess fat from leg of lamb. Using a sharp knife, cut several small slits on outside of lamb; stuff with garlic slices. Rub salt, pepper, and oregano over surface of lamb. Wrap lamb in heavy-duty aluminum foil. Insert meat thermometer through foil into lamb, making an opening so that thermometer does not touch foil, bone, or fat.

Prepare fire in a covered grill; let burn 15 to 20 minutes. Sprinkle wood chips over hot coals. Place leg of lamb on grill; cover with lid, and open vent. Grill over medium coals 2 hours or until thermometer registers 140° (rare) or 160° (medium). Let stand 10 minutes before slicing. Yield: about 10 servings.

GRILLED LAMB CHOPS

4 (1-inch-thick) lamb rib chops
2 tablespoons butter or margarine, softened
1½ teaspoons chopped fresh parsley
½ teaspoon salt
Dash of pepper
Dash of paprika
1 teaspoon lemon juice

Trim excess fat from chops. Combine softened butter, parsley, salt, pepper, and paprika in a small bowl, stirring until combined. Stir in lemon juice. Spread butter mixture evenly over chops.

Grill chops over medium coals 5 to 6 minutes on each side or until desired degree of doneness. Yield: 4 servings.

TERIYAKI LAMB CHOPS

6 (1-inch-thick) lamb sirloin chops
½ cup finely chopped onion
2 cloves garlic, sliced
¼ cup soy sauce
¼ cup cider vinegar
2 tablespoons honey
2 teaspoons ground ginger
¼ teaspoon dry mustard
¼ teaspoon pepper

Trim excess fat from chops, and place chops in a large shallow container. Combine remaining ingredients, stirring well; pour over chops. Cover and refrigerate at least 8 hours, turning chops occasionally.

Remove chops from marinade, reserving marinade. Grill over medium coals 8 to 10 minutes on each side or until desired degree of doneness. Baste frequently with marinade. Yield: 6 servings.

LAMB CHOPS WITH BÉARNAISE SAUCE

4 (1-inch-thick) lamb sirloin chops
2 tablespoons soy sauce
1 tablespoon catsup
1 tablespoon vegetable oil
½ teaspoon coarsely ground pepper
1 clove garlic, minced
Béarnaise sauce (recipe follows)

Trim excess fat from chops, and place chops in a large shallow container. Combine remaining ingredients except béarnaise sauce, stirring well; baste chops with soy sauce mixture. Cover and refrigerate at least 8 hours.

Grill chops over medium coals 5 to 8 minutes on each side or until desired degree of doneness. Serve with béarnaise sauce. Yield: 4 servings.

Béarnaise Sauce:

3 egg yolks
3 tablespoons tarragon vinegar
¼ teaspoon salt
¼ teaspoon coarsely ground pepper
⅔ cup butter or margarine, melted
2 tablespoons Chablis or other dry white wine
2 teaspoons minced green onions
1 teaspoon dried whole tarragon

Combine egg yolks, tarragon vinegar, salt, and coarsely ground pepper in container of an electric blender; cover and process 3 seconds at high speed. Turn blender to low speed, and add hot melted butter to yolk mixture in a slow, steady stream. Turn blender to high speed; cover and process until thick.

Combine wine, green onions, and tarragon in a small saucepan, stirring well. Cook over high heat until almost all liquid has evaporated. Add to mixture in blender; cover and process 4 seconds at high speed. Yield: 1⅓ cups.

BARBECUED LAMB CHOPS

8 (2-inch-thick) lamb rib chops
Salt and pepper to taste
3 cloves garlic, halved
½ cup red wine vinegar
¼ cup vegetable oil
Pinch of dried whole rosemary,
**   crushed**

Trim excess fat from lamb chops, and sprinkle chops with salt and pepper. Rub garlic over surface of chops. Combine red wine vinegar, vegetable oil, and crushed rosemary, stirring well; baste chops with vinegar mixture. Set remaining vinegar mixture aside.

Grill chops over medium coals 12 minutes on each side or until desired degree of doneness. Baste frequently with vinegar mixture. Yield: 8 servings.

OVEN-BARBECUED LAMB SHANKS

2 to 2½ pounds lamb shanks
½ cup all-purpose flour
¼ cup shortening, melted
1 teaspoon salt
¼ teaspoon pepper
1 cup water
1 medium onion, finely chopped
½ cup raisins
½ cup vinegar
¼ cup catsup
8 pitted prunes
2 tablespoons brown sugar
2 tablespoons Worcestershire
**   sauce**

Dredge lamb shanks in flour, coating well. Sauté lamb in shortening in a large skillet over medium heat until browned. Drain on paper towels.

Place lamb in a lightly greased 2½-quart shallow baking dish; sprinkle with salt and pepper.

Combine remaining ingredients, stirring well; pour over lamb. Cover and bake at 300° for 2 hours or until tender. Yield: 4 servings.

LAMB KABOBS

1½ pounds boneless lamb, cut into
**   1-inch cubes**
¼ cup plus 2 tablespoons white
**   wine vinegar**
¼ cup plus 2 tablespoons water
2 tablespoons chopped fresh parsley
1 tablespoon plus 1½ teaspoons
**   sugar**
1 tablespoon dried whole rosemary,
**   crushed**
2 tablespoons dry sherry
½ teaspoon salt
¼ teaspoon pepper
6 large fresh mushroom caps

Place lamb cubes in a large shallow container. Combine remaining ingredients except mushrooms, stirring well; pour marinade over lamb. Cover and refrigerate at least 2 hours, stirring lamb occasionally.

Remove lamb from marinade, reserving marinade. Place ½ cup marinade in a small saucepan; set aside. Reserve remaining marinade for basting. Thread lamb on 6 skewers. Grill over medium coals 15 to 20 minutes or until desired degree of doneness. Turn and baste frequently with reserved marinade.

Add mushroom caps to marinade in saucepan; bring to a boil. Reduce heat, and simmer, uncovered, 4 to 5 minutes. Drain. Thread a mushroom cap on each skewer. Yield: 6 servings.

SHISH KABOBS TERIYAKI

1 pound boneless lamb, cut into 1-inch
  cubes
¼ cup soy sauce
¼ cup vinegar
¼ cup vegetable oil
1 clove garlic, minced
¼ teaspoon ground ginger
4 cherry tomatoes
1 medium-size green pepper, cut into
  1-inch pieces
1 (8-ounce) can pineapple chunks,
  drained
1 (8-ounce) can whole water chestnuts,
  drained

Place lamb cubes in a large shallow
container. Combine soy sauce, vinegar,
oil, garlic, and ginger, stirring well; pour
over lamb. Cover and refrigerate at least 8
hours, stirring lamb occasionally.

Remove lamb from marinade, reserving
marinade. Alternate lamb, tomatoes,
green pepper, pineapple, and water
chestnuts on skewers. Grill over medium
coals 10 minutes on each side or until
desired degree of doneness. Baste frequently with marinade. Yield: 4 servings.

OVERNIGHT SHISH KABOBS

2 pounds boneless lamb, cut into 1-inch
  cubes
1 onion, finely diced
½ cup Burgundy or other dry red wine
⅓ cup finely diced green pepper
¼ cup olive oil
½ teaspoon pepper
¼ teaspoon rubbed sage
⅛ teaspoon dry mustard
⅛ teaspoon dried whole oregano

Place lamb in a large shallow container.
Combine remaining ingredients, stirring

well; pour over lamb. Cover and refrigerate at least 8 hours, stirring lamb occasionally.

Remove lamb from marinade, reserving
marinade. Transfer marinade to a small
saucepan, and cook over medium heat
until thoroughly heated, stirring constantly. Remove marinade from heat; set
aside and keep warm.

Thread lamb on skewers, and grill over
medium coals 15 to 20 minutes or until
desired degree of doneness. Turn and
baste frequently with marinade. Yield: 6
to 8 servings.

SHISH KABOBS

2 pounds boneless lamb, cut into
  1½-inch cubes
½ cup diced onion
1 small clove garlic, minced
½ cup olive oil
¼ cup Burgundy or other dry red wine
½ teaspoon salt
½ teaspoon dried whole oregano
⅛ teaspoon freshly ground pepper
Dash of red pepper
1 medium onion, cut into 1-inch pieces
1 medium-size green pepper, cut into
  1-inch pieces
8 cherry tomatoes

Place lamb cubes in a large shallow
container. Combine diced onion and next
7 ingredients, stirring mixture well; pour
over lamb cubes. Cover and marinate in
refrigerator at least 8 hours, stirring lamb
occasionally.

Remove lamb from marinade, reserving
marinade. Alternate lamb and vegetables
on skewers. Grill kabobs over medium
coals 15 to 20 minutes or until desired
degree of doneness. Turn and baste frequently with marinade. Yield: 8 servings.

Pork

BARBECUED LEG OF PORK

1 (14- to 16-pound) leg of pork
Fiery Barbecue Sauce

Insert meat thermometer into leg of pork, making sure it does not touch bone or fat. Prepare fire in a covered grill. Place pork on grill. Cover and cook over low coals 4½ hours; turn occasionally. Baste with sauce. Cover and cook 2 hours or until thermometer registers 160° (medium). Baste frequently with sauce. Let stand 10 to 15 minutes before slicing. Serve with sauce. Yield: 20 to 25 servings.

Fiery Barbecue Sauce:

1 cup water
¾ cup firmly packed brown sugar
¾ cup catsup
½ cup vinegar
½ cup Worcestershire sauce
½ cup butter or margarine
¼ cup lemon juice
1 tablespoon salt
1 tablespoon plus 1 teaspoon dry mustard
1 tablespoon plus 1 teaspoon chili powder
1 tablespoon plus 1 teaspoon paprika
2 teaspoons red pepper

Combine all ingredients in a large saucepan; stir well. Cook, uncovered, over medium heat until sugar dissolves, stirring frequently. Yield: about 4 cups.

BARBECUED PORK SHOULDER

1 (6- to 7-pound) pork shoulder roast
1 medium onion, minced
1 clove garlic, minced
½ cup butter or margarine, melted
1 cup firmly packed brown sugar
1 cup catsup
½ cup vinegar
½ cup water
2 tablespoons Worcestershire sauce
1½ teaspoons grated lemon rind
1 tablespoon plus 1½ teaspoons lemon juice
1 teaspoon hot sauce
½ teaspoon chili powder

Insert meat thermometer into thickest part of roast, making sure it does not touch bone or fat. Sauté onion and garlic in butter in a medium saucepan until tender. Stir in remaining ingredients; bring to a boil. Reduce heat, and simmer, uncovered, 5 minutes, stirring occasionally. Remove sauce from heat. Set roast and sauce aside.

Prepare fire in a covered grill. Place roast on grill. Cover with lid, and open vent. Cook over low coals 3 hours, turning roast occasionally. Baste roast with sauce. Cover and cook an additional hour or until thermometer registers 160° (medium). Baste frequently with remaining sauce. Let stand 10 to 15 minutes before slicing. Yield: 10 to 12 servings.

SLICED BARBECUED PORK

4 cups catsup
2 cups vinegar
2 tablespoons plus ¼ teaspoon lemon juice
1 tablespoon hot sauce
1½ teaspoons Worcestershire sauce
½ teaspoon olive oil
½ teaspoon prepared mustard
¼ teaspoon garlic salt
½ cup cider vinegar
¾ teaspoon hot sauce
1 (5- to 5½-pound) pork shoulder roast

Combine first 8 ingredients in a small Dutch oven, stirring well. Cook, uncovered, over low heat 1 hour, stirring occasionally. Remove sauce from heat. Set sauce aside.

Combine cider vinegar and ¾ teaspoon hot sauce, stirring well. Set vinegar mixture aside.

Insert meat thermometer into thickest part of roast, making sure it does not touch bone or fat. Grill roast over low coals 6 to 7 hours or until thermometer registers 160° (medium). Turn and baste frequently with vinegar mixture. Baste roast with sauce during last hour of grilling time. Let stand 10 to 15 minutes before slicing.

Slice pork roast thinly, and toss with enough sauce to coat well. If desired, cover and refrigerate remaining sauce for later use. Yield: about 8 servings.

LOUISIANA-STYLE SPIT-ROASTED PORK

1 (6½- to 7-pound) boneless pork loin roast, rolled and tied
1 cup soy sauce
1 cup Burgundy or other dry red wine
½ cup cider vinegar
¼ cup lemon juice
½ teaspoon prepared mustard
3 cloves garlic, minced

Place roast in a zip-top heavy-duty plastic bag. Combine remaining ingredients, stirring well; pour over roast, and secure bag tightly. Place bag in a large shallow container; refrigerate at least 8 hours, turning bag occasionally.

Remove roast from marinade, reserving marinade. Thread roast on spit; secure with prongs at each end of spit. Balance roast properly to avoid strain on motor. Insert meat thermometer into thickest part of roast, making sure it does not touch fat or spit. Place spit on rotisserie 3 to 4 inches from low coals. Grill 2½ to 3 hours or until thermometer registers 160° (medium). Baste with marinade during last hour of grilling time. Remove roast from spit; let stand 10 to 15 minutes before slicing. Yield: about 16 servings.

OVEN-BARBECUED CRANBERRY PORK ROAST

4 cups fresh cranberries
1 cup sugar
½ cup commercial barbecue sauce or see Sauce chapter
½ cup orange juice
1 (4- to 6-pound) pork loin roast

Wash and sort cranberries; drain well. Combine cranberries, sugar, sauce, and juice in a large saucepan, stirring well; bring to a boil, stirring constantly. Boil, without stirring, 5 minutes. Remove cranberry mixture from heat, and set aside.

Place roast, fat side up, on a rack in a shallow roasting pan. Insert meat thermometer into thickest part of roast, making sure it does not touch bone or fat. Bake at 325° for 3 to 3½ hours or until thermometer registers 160° (medium). Baste frequently with cranberry mixture during last 30 minutes of baking time. Let stand 10 to 15 minutes before slicing. Serve roast with remaining cranberry mixture. Yield: 6 to 10 servings.

MARINATED PORK TENDERLOIN

2 (¾-pound) pork tenderloins, trimmed
1 (15-ounce) can unsweetened sliced
 pineapple, undrained
2 tablespoons minced fresh gingerroot
2 tablespoons soy sauce
2 cloves garlic, minced
½ teaspoon dry mustard

Place tenderloins in a large shallow container. Drain pineapple, reserving juice; set pineapple slices aside. Combine juice, gingerroot, soy sauce, garlic, and mustard, stirring well; pour over tenderloins. Cover and refrigerate at least 8 hours, turning tenderloins occasionally.

Remove tenderloins from marinade. Insert meat thermometer into one tenderloin, making sure it does not touch fat. Grill over medium coals 50 to 55 minutes or until thermometer registers 160° (medium). Turn tenderloins occasionally. Let stand 10 to 15 minutes before slicing.

Grill pineapple over medium coals 1 minute on each side. Slice tenderloins; serve with pineapple. Yield: 6 servings.

MARINATED PORK STEAKS

4 (¾-inch-thick) pork blade steaks
1 (8¼-ounce) can sliced pineapple,
 undrained
1 medium onion, chopped
½ cup soy sauce
¼ cup vegetable oil
3 tablespoons light corn syrup
1 teaspoon ground ginger

Trim excess fat from steaks, and place steaks in a large shallow container. Drain pineapple, reserving syrup; set pineapple slices aside. Combine pineapple syrup, onion, soy sauce, oil, corn syrup, and ginger in a small saucepan, stirring well. Cook, uncovered, over medium heat 10 minutes, stirring frequently; pour over steaks. Cover and refrigerate at least 8 hours, turning steaks occasionally.

Remove steaks from marinade, reserving marinade. Grill steaks over low to medium coals 35 minutes or until desired degree of doneness. Turn and baste occasionally with marinade.

Grill reserved pineapple slices over medium coals 1 minute on each side. Garnish pork steaks with pineapple slices. Yield: 4 servings.

BARBECUED HAM

1 cup unsweetened pineapple juice
¼ cup plus 1 tablespoon firmly packed
 brown sugar
1 tablespoon dry mustard
2 tablespoons lemon juice
1 teaspoon onion salt
2 teaspoons soy sauce
2 (½-inch-thick) slices smoked ham
 (about ¾ pound)
1 (8¼-ounce) can sliced pineapple,
 drained

Combine first 6 ingredients in a medium saucepan, stirring well; bring to a boil. Reduce heat, and simmer, uncovered, 5 minutes; stir frequently. Remove sauce from heat, and set aside.

Trim excess fat from ham slices. Grill over medium coals 20 to 25 minutes or until desired degree of doneness. Turn ham slices and baste every 5 minutes with reserved sauce.

Grill pineapple slices over medium coals 1 minute on each side. Garnish ham with pineapple, and serve with remaining sauce. Yield: about 4 servings.

COUNTRY-PRIDE PORK CHOPS

4 (1-inch-thick) center-cut pork chops
½ cup soy sauce
¼ cup firmly packed brown sugar
¼ cup sherry
1 teaspoon ground cinnamon
½ teaspoon garlic salt
Dash of ground ginger

Trim excess fat from pork chops, and place chops in a large shallow container. Combine remaining ingredients, stirring well; pour over chops. Cover and marinate in refrigerator at least 8 hours, turning frequently.

Remove chops from marinade, reserving marinade. Grill chops over medium coals 15 minutes on each side or until desired degree of doneness. Baste frequently with marinade. Yield: 4 servings.

MARINATED BARBECUED PORK CHOPS

6 to 8 (1-inch-thick) pork loin or
  rib chops
½ cup vegetable oil
¼ cup olive oil
¼ cup lemon juice
1 tablespoon salt
1 teaspoon paprika
½ teaspoon pepper
6 bay leaves, halved
3 cloves garlic, crushed

Trim excess fat from pork chops, and place chops in a large shallow container. Combine remaining ingredients, stirring well; pour over chops. Cover and refrigerate at least 8 hours, turning once.

Remove pork chops from marinade, reserving marinade. Grill over medium coals 40 to 45 minutes or until desired degree of doneness. Turn and baste occasionally with reserved marinade. Yield: 6 to 8 servings.

BARBECUED PORK CHOPS

1½ cups water
¾ cup catsup
¾ cup vinegar
1 medium onion, chopped
1 clove garlic, minced
3 tablespoons brown sugar
1 tablespoon Worcestershire sauce
2 teaspoons salt
½ teaspoon pepper
¼ teaspoon hot sauce
8 (1¼-inch-thick) pork loin chops

Combine first 10 ingredients in a medium saucepan, stirring well; bring to a boil. Reduce heat, and simmer, uncovered, 30 minutes, stirring occasionally. Remove sauce from heat; set aside.

Trim excess fat from chops. Grill over medium coals 15 minutes on each side or until desired degree of doneness. Baste frequently with sauce. Serve pork chops with remaining sauce. Yield: 8 servings.

GRILLED PORK CHOPS

¼ cup lemon juice
¼ cup butter or margarine
2 tablespoons Worcestershire sauce
¼ teaspoon salt
¼ teaspoon pepper
4 (1-inch-thick) pork chops

Combine all ingredients except chops in a small saucepan, stirring well; bring to a boil. Reduce heat, and simmer, uncovered, 15 minutes; stir occasionally. Remove sauce from heat; set aside.

Trim excess fat from pork chops. Grill over hot coals 20 minutes on each side or until desired degree of doneness. Baste frequently with sauce. Yield: 4 servings.

HICKORY-SMOKED STUFFED PORK CHOPS

Hickory chips
½ cup chopped onion
½ cup chopped celery
¼ cup butter or margarine, melted
1 cup herb-seasoned dressing mix
⅓ cup water
¼ teaspoon salt
¼ teaspoon pepper
4 (1½-inch-thick) pork loin chops
Liquid smoke

Soak hickory chips in water to cover for at least 1 hour. Drain.

Sauté onion and celery in butter in a medium saucepan until tender. Add dressing mix, water, salt, and pepper, stirring well. Remove dressing mixture from heat, and set aside.

Trim excess fat from pork chops; make pockets in chops, cutting from rib side just to beginning of fat edge of each chop. Stuff pockets of chops with dressing mixture, and secure with wooden picks. Set aside.

Prepare fire in a covered grill; let burn until coals are gray. Rake coals to one end of grill; place wood chips over hot coals. Place chops at opposite end; cover with lid. Grill over indirect heat 1 hour or until desired degree of doneness. Turn and sprinkle with liquid smoke every 15 minutes. Yield: 4 servings.

HAWAIIAN GRILLED PORK CHOPS

1 (20-ounce) can sliced pineapple, undrained
6 (1-inch-thick) pork chops
½ cup soy sauce
⅓ cup vegetable oil
¼ cup minced onion
1 clove garlic, minced
1 tablespoon brown sugar

Drain pineapple, reserving ¼ cup syrup. Set pineapple slices aside.

Trim excess fat from pork chops, and place chops in a large shallow container. Combine pineapple syrup, soy sauce, oil, onion, garlic, and sugar, stirring well; pour over chops. Cover and refrigerate at least 2 hours, turning once.

Remove chops from marinade, reserving marinade. Grill over medium coals 40 to 45 minutes or until desired degree of doneness. Turn and baste frequently with marinade. Place a pineapple slice on each chop during last few minutes of grilling time. Yield: 6 servings.

OVEN-BARBECUED PORK CHOPS

6 (¾- to 1-inch-thick) pork chops
2 cups soy sauce
1 cup water
½ cup firmly packed brown sugar
1 tablespoon molasses
1 teaspoon salt
1 (14-ounce) bottle catsup
1 (12-ounce) bottle chili sauce
½ cup firmly packed brown sugar
⅓ cup water
1 tablespoon dry mustard

Trim excess fat from pork chops, and place chops in a large shallow container. Combine soy sauce, 1 cup water, ½ cup brown sugar, molasses, and salt, stirring well; pour over chops. Cover and refrigerate at least 8 hours, turning chops once.

Remove chops from marinade, and transfer to a 13- x 9- x 2-inch baking pan. Cover and bake at 350° for 1½ hours.

Combine catsup, chili sauce, ½ cup brown sugar, ⅓ cup water, and dry mustard in a large saucepan; bring to a boil, stirring constantly. Remove sauce from heat, and pour over pork chops; bake, uncovered, an additional 20 to 25 minutes or until tender. Serve pork chops with sauce. Yield: 6 servings.

OVEN-BARBECUED SPARERIBS

4 pounds spareribs
1 tablespoon plus 1½ teaspoons lemon-pepper seasoning
½ cup catsup
½ cup commercial hot barbecue sauce or see Sauce chapter
1 (6-ounce) can frozen orange juice concentrate, thawed and undiluted
¼ cup butter or margarine
2 tablespoons brown sugar
1 tablespoon soy sauce
2 teaspoons prepared mustard
4 to 5 green onions, finely chopped

Cut ribs into serving-size pieces, and sprinkle with lemon-pepper seasoning. Place ribs in a single layer in a large shallow baking dish. Cover and bake at 350° for 45 minutes.

Combine remaining ingredients in a medium saucepan, stirring well; bring to a boil. Reduce heat, and simmer sauce, uncovered, 10 minutes, stirring occasionally. Remove ribs from oven, and baste with sauce. Cover and bake an additional 45 minutes. Turn and baste occasionally with remaining sauce. Yield: 4 servings.

PEACHTREE RIBS

4 pounds spareribs
1 (7¾-ounce) jar strained junior peaches
½ cup firmly packed brown sugar
⅓ cup catsup
⅓ cup vinegar
2 tablespoons soy sauce
1 teaspoon ground ginger
2 cloves garlic, minced

Cut ribs into serving-size pieces; place in a large Dutch oven. Add water to cover; bring to a boil. Cover, reduce heat, and simmer 40 to 50 minutes. Drain ribs, and place in a large shallow container. Combine remaining ingredients, stirring well; pour over ribs. Cover and refrigerate at least 8 hours, turning once.

Remove ribs from marinade, reserving marinade. Grill over hot coals 40 to 50 minutes or until desired degree of doneness. Turn and baste frequently with marinade. Yield: 4 servings.

APPLE-BARBECUED RIBS

6 pounds spareribs
½ cup chopped onion
1 clove garlic, minced
¼ cup vegetable oil
1 (16-ounce) can applesauce
½ cup catsup
⅓ cup chopped fresh parsley
2 tablespoons honey
2 tablespoons lemon juice
1 tablespoon Worcestershire sauce
1 teaspoon salt
1 teaspoon prepared mustard
½ teaspoon ground ginger
¼ teaspoon pepper

Cut ribs into serving-size pieces, and place in a large Dutch oven. Add water to cover; bring to a boil. Cover, reduce heat, and simmer 30 minutes. Drain ribs, and set aside.

Sauté onion and garlic in oil in a medium saucepan until tender. Stir in remaining ingredients; bring to a boil. Reduce heat, and simmer, uncovered, 15 minutes, stirring occasionally. Remove sauce from heat, and set aside.

Grill ribs over low coals 40 minutes, turning frequently. Baste ribs with sauce. Grill an additional 20 minutes or until desired degree of doneness. Turn and baste frequently with sauce. Serve ribs with remaining sauce. Yield: 6 servings.

SPIT-ROASTED SPARERIBS

1 cup commercial barbecue sauce
  or see Sauce chapter
½ cup water
¼ cup molasses
¼ cup vinegar
3 tablespoons Worcestershire sauce
2 teaspoons salt
½ teaspoon dry mustard
¼ teaspoon pepper
2 cloves garlic, minced
4 pounds spareribs

Combine all ingredients except spareribs, stirring well. Set sauce aside.

Cut ribs into serving-size pieces, and thread on spit; secure with prongs at each end of spit. Balance ribs properly to avoid strain on motor. Place spit on rotisserie 3 to 4 inches from low coals. Grill ribs 1 hour or until desired degree of doneness. Baste with sauce during last 20 minutes of grilling time. Yield: 4 servings.

COUNTRY-STYLE RIBS

4 pounds country-style spareribs
1 onion, sliced
3 tablespoons butter or margarine
¼ cup finely chopped onion
1 clove garlic, minced
1 cup catsup
½ cup cider vinegar
Juice of ½ lemon
1 tablespoon sugar
2 tablespoons Worcestershire sauce
2 teaspoons prepared mustard
½ teaspoon salt
¼ teaspoon pepper

Cut ribs into 6 serving-size pieces, and place in a large Dutch oven. Add sliced onion and water to cover ribs; bring to a boil. Cover, reduce heat, and simmer 45 minutes. Drain ribs, and set aside.

Melt butter in a medium saucepan over low heat. Add chopped onion and garlic;

sauté until tender. Stir in remaining ingredients; bring to a boil. Remove sauce from heat, and set aside.

Grill ribs over medium coals 20 to 30 minutes or until desired degree of doneness. Turn and baste frequently with sauce. Yield: 6 servings.

TANGY BARBECUED COUNTRY-STYLE RIBS

¼ cup chopped onion
2 tablespoons vegetable oil
1 cup chili sauce
½ cup tomato juice
¼ cup firmly packed brown sugar
¼ cup lemon juice
2 tablespoons Worcestershire sauce
6 drops of hot sauce
3 pounds country-style spareribs or
  backbones
Salt and pepper to taste

Sauté onion in oil in a small saucepan until tender. Stir in chili sauce, tomato juice, sugar, lemon juice, Worcestershire sauce, and hot sauce; bring to a boil. Reduce heat, and simmer, uncovered, 20 minutes, stirring occasionally. Remove sauce from heat, and set aside.

Cut country-style ribs into 4 serving-size pieces, and sprinkle with salt and pepper to taste. Grill over low coals 45 minutes to 1 hour or until desired degree of doneness, turning frequently. Baste ribs with sauce during last 20 minutes of grilling time. Serve with remaining sauce. Yield: about 4 servings.

PORK KABOBS

**2 pounds boneless pork, cut into
  1-inch cubes**
½ cup olive oil
¼ cup red wine vinegar
2 tablespoons soy sauce
1 teaspoon dry mustard
½ teaspoon celery seeds
½ teaspoon dried whole rosemary
½ teaspoon rubbed sage
Dash of pepper
2 cloves garlic, minced

Place pork cubes in a large shallow container. Combine remaining ingredients, stirring well; pour over pork. Cover and refrigerate at least 8 hours, stirring pork occasionally.

Remove pork from marinade, reserving marinade. Thread pork on skewers. Grill kabobs over medium coals 30 minutes or until desired degree of doneness, turning frequently. Baste kabobs with marinade during last 10 minutes of grilling time. Yield: 6 to 8 servings.

SWISS-HAM KABOBS

**1 (20-ounce) can unsweetened
  pineapple chunks, undrained**
½ cup orange marmalade
1 tablespoon prepared mustard
¼ teaspoon ground cloves
1 pound fully cooked ham
½ pound Swiss cheese

Drain pineapple, reserving 2 tablespoons juice. Set chunks aside. Combine juice, orange marmalade, mustard, and cloves, stirring well. Set sauce aside.

Cut ham and Swiss cheese into 1½- x ½- x ½-inch pieces. Thread ham, cheese, ham, then pineapple chunks on skewers (cheese must be between and touching ham to prevent rapid melting).

Baste kabobs with reserved sauce, and grill over hot coals 3 to 4 minutes or until cheese is partially melted and ham is lightly browned. Turn and baste frequently with remaining sauce. Yield: 6 servings.

SOUTHERN TENDER KABOBS

**2½ to 3 pounds boneless pork, cut into
  1½-inch cubes**
½ cup soy sauce
¼ cup firmly packed brown sugar
2 tablespoons sherry
½ teaspoon garlic powder
½ teaspoon ground cinnamon
1 (12-ounce) jar red currant jelly
1 tablespoon prepared mustard
2 small tomatoes, quartered
2 small onions, peeled and quartered
**1 medium-size green pepper, cut into
  1-inch pieces**
½ pound fresh mushrooms

Place pork cubes in a large shallow container. Combine soy sauce, brown sugar, sherry, garlic powder, and cinnamon, stirring well; pour over pork. Cover and marinate in refrigerator at least 4 hours, stirring pork occasionally.

Combine red currant jelly and mustard in a small saucepan; bring to a boil, stirring until jelly dissolves and mixture is blended. Remove jelly mixture from heat, and set aside.

Remove pork cubes from marinade. Thread pork on skewers. Alternate vegetables on separate skewers. Grill pork kabobs over medium coals 20 minutes, turning frequently. Place vegetable kabobs on grill. Grill vegetable and pork kabobs an additional 10 to 15 minutes or until desired degree of doneness. Turn and baste kabobs frequently with jelly mixture. Yield: about 8 servings.

Poultry

OVEN-BARBECUED TURKEY

1 (10- to 11-pound) turkey
2 tablespoons olive oil
2 teaspoons salt
2 teaspoons pepper
Barbecue sauce (recipe follows)

Remove giblets and neck from turkey (reserve for use in other recipes). Rinse turkey thoroughly with cold water, and pat dry. Rub olive oil over surface of turkey. Sprinkle salt and pepper over surface and in cavity of turkey.

Close cavity of turkey with wooden picks. Tie ends of legs to tail with string or tuck them under band of skin at tail. Fold neck skin over back, and secure with wooden picks. Lift wingtips up and over back, and tuck under turkey.

Place turkey, breast side up, in a deep roasting pan. Insert meat thermometer into breast or meaty part of thigh, making sure it does not touch bone or fat. Bake, uncovered, at 350° for 2 hours. Baste frequently with pan drippings. Cut the cord or band of skin holding the drumstick ends to the tail (this will ensure that the insides of thighs are cooked). Pour barbecue sauce over turkey.

Cover turkey and bake an additional hour or until thermometer registers 185°. Baste frequently with sauce. Turkey is done when drumsticks are easy to move. Let stand 10 to 15 minutes before slicing. Yield: 10 to 12 servings.

Barbecue Sauce:

1 (14½-ounce) can whole tomatoes, undrained
1 medium onion, sliced
2 cloves garlic, minced
3 fresh celery leaves, chopped
1 bay leaf
1 teaspoon sugar
1 teaspoon salt
¼ teaspoon chili powder
¼ teaspoon paprika
⅛ teaspoon dried whole thyme
⅛ teaspoon dried whole basil
1 medium onion, chopped
1 medium-size green pepper, chopped
2 tablespoons olive oil
1 whole pimiento, chopped
1 tablespoon all-purpose flour
4 drops of hot sauce
Dash of soy sauce

Combine first 11 ingredients in a Dutch oven, stirring well; bring to a boil. Cover, reduce heat, and simmer 25 minutes or until vegetables are tender. Remove from heat, and process mixture through a food mill. Return tomato mixture to Dutch oven, and set aside.

Sauté chopped onion and green pepper in olive oil in a large heavy skillet until tender; add remaining ingredients, stirring well. Add to tomato mixture in Dutch oven, stirring until combined. Yield: about 2 quarts.

LEMON-BARBECUED TURKEY

1 (10- to 10½-pound) turkey, quartered
4 small cloves garlic, crushed
2 teaspoons salt
1¾ cups lemon juice
1 cup vegetable oil
½ cup chopped onion
2 teaspoons ground thyme
2 teaspoons pepper

Place turkey in a large shallow container. Mash garlic with salt in a medium bowl, using a fork. Add remaining ingredients, stirring well; pour over turkey. Cover and refrigerate at least 8 hours, turning turkey occasionally.

Remove turkey from marinade, reserving marinade. Prepare fire in a covered grill. Place turkey, skin side down, on grill. Cover with lid, and grill over medium coals 2 hours or until done, turning every 15 minutes. Baste turkey with marinade during last 30 minutes of grilling time. Let stand 10 to 15 minutes before slicing. Yield: about 10 servings.

BARBECUED CHICKEN

Mesquite or oak chips
2 (2½- to 3-pound) broiler-fryers
1 tablespoon lemon-pepper seasoning
1 tablespoon seasoned pepper
¼ teaspoon garlic powder
3 cups commercial barbecue sauce or
see Sauce chapter

Soak mesquite chips in water to cover for at least 1 hour. Drain.

Remove giblets and necks from cavities of chickens (reserve for use in other recipes). Rinse chickens thoroughly with cold water; pat dry. Fold neck skin over backs; secure with wooden picks. Lift wingtips up and over backs; tuck under chickens. Close cavities, and secure with wooden picks; truss chickens. Insert meat thermometer into breast or meaty part of thigh of one chicken, making sure it does

not touch bone or fat. Combine lemon-pepper seasoning, pepper, and garlic powder, stirring well; sprinkle over chickens. Set chickens aside.

Prepare fire in a covered grill; let burn until coals are gray. Rake coals to one end of grill; place wood chips over hot coals. Place chickens at opposite end; cover with lid. Grill over indirect heat 45 minutes. Baste with sauce, and grill an additional hour and 45 minutes or until thermometer registers 185°. Baste every 30 minutes with remaining sauce. Let stand 10 to 15 minutes before slicing. Yield: 8 servings.

CORNISH HENS ITALIANO

½ cup butter or margarine
½ cup lime juice
¼ cup vegetable oil
2 (0.7-ounce) envelopes dry Italian
salad dressing mix
4 (1- to 1¼-pound) Cornish hens

Combine first 4 ingredients in a saucepan; stir well. Bring to a boil. Reduce heat, and simmer, uncovered, 5 minutes. Remove sauce from heat; keep warm.

Remove giblets from Cornish hens (reserve for use in other recipes). Rinse hens thoroughly with cold water; pat dry. Fold neck skin over backs; secure with wooden picks. Lift wingtips up and over backs; tuck under hens. Close cavities, and secure with wooden picks; truss hens. Thread hens on spit; secure with prongs at each end of spit. Balance hens properly to avoid strain on motor. Insert meat thermometer into breast or meaty part of thigh of one hen, making sure it does not touch bone or spit. Place spit on rotisserie 4 to 6 inches from medium coals. Grill hens 1 hour and 15 minutes or until thermometer registers 185°. Baste frequently with sauce. Remove hens from spit; let stand 10 to 15 minutes before slicing. Yield: 4 servings.

TEXAS-STYLE GAME HENS

½ cup apple jelly
½ cup catsup
1 tablespoon vinegar
½ teaspoon chili powder
½ teaspoon salt
½ teaspoon garlic powder
½ teaspoon chili powder
4 (1- to 1¼-pound) Cornish hens, split

Combine first 4 ingredients in a small saucepan; stir well. Cook over medium heat until jelly melts, stirring constantly. Remove sauce from heat; keep warm.

Combine salt, garlic powder, and ½ teaspoon chili powder, stirring well; sprinkle over Cornish hens. Grill over medium coals 45 minutes; turn occasionally. Baste with sauce. Grill an additional 15 minutes. Turn and baste frequently with remaining sauce. Let stand 10 to 15 minutes before slicing. Yield: 4 servings.

HONEY-BARBECUED CHICKEN

1 (2½- to 3-pound) broiler-fryer, split
¾ cup butter or margarine, melted
⅓ cup vinegar
¼ cup honey
2 cloves garlic, minced
2 teaspoons salt
½ teaspoon dry mustard
Dash of pepper

Place chicken in a large shallow container. Combine remaining ingredients, stirring sauce well. Grill chicken, skin side up, over hot coals 30 to 35 minutes or until done. Turn and baste frequently with sauce. Yield: 4 servings.

SAUCY CHICKEN

2 (2½- to 3-pound) broiler-fryers, split
1 cup vegetable oil
½ cup vinegar
¼ cup chili sauce
1 tablespoon prepared horseradish
1 teaspoon salt
½ teaspoon dry mustard
1 small clove garlic, crushed

Place chicken in 2 large shallow containers. Combine remaining ingredients, stirring well; pour over chicken. Cover and refrigerate at least 2 hours, turning chicken occasionally.

Remove chicken from marinade, reserving marinade. Grill chicken over low coals 45 minutes or until done. Turn and baste chicken frequently with marinade. Yield: 8 servings.

LEMON-BARBECUED CHICKEN

2 (2½- to 3-pound) broiler-fryers, split
1 cup vegetable oil
½ cup lemon juice
1 tablespoon salt
2 teaspoons onion powder
2 teaspoons dried whole basil
1 teaspoon paprika
½ teaspoon dried whole thyme
1 clove garlic, crushed
1 lemon, sliced

Place chicken in 2 large shallow containers. Combine remaining ingredients, stirring well; pour over chicken. Cover and refrigerate at least 8 hours, turning chicken occasionally.

Remove chicken from marinade, reserving marinade. Grill chicken, skin side up, over low coals 20 to 25 minutes. Baste frequently with marinade. Turn chicken, and grill an additional 20 minutes or until done. Yield: 8 servings.

OUTDOOR BARBECUED CHICKEN

2 cloves garlic
1 teaspoon salt
½ cup vegetable oil
½ cup lemon juice or vinegar
½ cup water
¼ cup finely grated onion
1 teaspoon pepper
2 teaspoons Worcestershire sauce
2 (2½- to 3-pound) broiler-fryers, split

Mash garlic with salt in a small bowl, using a fork; stir in remaining ingredients except chicken. Cover and refrigerate sauce 24 hours.

Grill chicken over low coals 45 minutes or until done. Turn and baste frequently with sauce. Yield: 8 servings.

EASY BARBECUED CHICKEN

Hickory chips
2 tablespoons salt
2 tablespoons paprika
1½ teaspoons pepper
4 (3- to 3½-pound) broiler-fryers, split
3 tablespoons vegetable oil
1 tablespoon vinegar
1 teaspoon hot sauce

Soak hickory chips in water to cover for at least 1 hour. Drain.

Combine salt, paprika, and pepper, stirring well; sprinkle over chicken. Combine vegetable oil, vinegar, and hot sauce, stirring well. Set chicken and oil mixture aside.

Prepare fire in a covered grill; let burn until coals are gray. Rake coals to one end of grill; place wood chips over hot coals. Place chicken at opposite end of grill, and cover with lid. Grill over indirect heat 3 to 3½ hours or until done, turning chicken occasionally. Baste chicken with oil mixture during last hour of grilling time. Yield: 16 servings.

BACKYARD BARBECUED CHICKEN

2 cups butter or margarine
¾ cup vinegar
3 tablespoons plus 1½ teaspoons dry mustard
2 (3- to 3½-pound) broiler-fryers, split
2 teaspoons salt

Combine butter, vinegar, and dry mustard in a medium saucepan; bring to a boil. Reduce heat, and simmer, uncovered, 5 minutes or until butter melts, stirring frequently. Remove sauce from heat, and keep warm.

Sprinkle chicken with salt. Grill chicken, skin side down, over low heat 1 hour and 15 minutes or until done, turning occasionally. Baste chicken frequently with reserved warm butter sauce. Yield: 8 servings.

MARINATED BARBECUED CHICKEN

1 (2½- to 3-pound) broiler-fryer, quartered
1 (8-ounce) can tomato sauce
½ cup olive oil
½ cup orange juice
¼ cup vinegar
1 teaspoon salt
1½ teaspoons dried whole oregano
¼ teaspoon pepper
1 clove garlic, minced

Place chicken in a large shallow container. Combine remaining ingredients in a jar; cover tightly, and shake vigorously. Pour marinade over chicken. Cover and refrigerate at least 8 hours, turning chicken occasionally.

Remove chicken from marinade, reserving marinade. Grill chicken over medium coals 50 to 60 minutes or until done. Turn and baste every 15 minutes with marinade. Yield: 4 servings.

BARBECUED CRANBERRY CHICKEN

1 chicken-flavored bouillon cube
½ cup boiling water
1 (16-ounce) can whole berry
  cranberry sauce
1 cup chili sauce
Juice of 1 small lemon
1 tablespoon instant minced
  onion
1 tablespoon Worcestershire
  sauce
1 teaspoon dry mustard
2 (3- to 3½-pound) broiler-fryers,
  quartered
Salt and pepper to taste

Dissolve bouillon cube in water; combine with next 6 ingredients in container of an electric blender. Cover; process until sauce is smooth. Set aside.

Sprinkle chicken with salt and pepper. Grill chicken, skin side down, over hot coals 30 minutes, turning every 10 minutes. Baste chicken with sauce. Grill an additional 30 minutes. Baste every 10 minutes with sauce. Serve chicken with remaining sauce. Yield: 8 servings.

GRILLED BARBECUED CHICKEN

1 cup red wine vinegar
½ cup vegetable oil
1½ teaspoons hot sauce
Dash of garlic salt
1 (2½- to 3-pound) broiler-fryer,
  quartered
Salt to taste

Combine red wine vinegar, vegetable oil, and hot sauce in a jar; cover tightly, and shake sauce vigorously. Sprinkle chicken with salt to taste; baste with sauce. Grill chicken, skin side down, over medium coals 50 to 60 minutes or until done. Turn and baste every 10 minutes with sauce. Yield: 4 servings.

OLD SOUTH ZESTY BARBECUED CHICKEN

1 cup vegetable oil
½ cup vinegar
½ teaspoon salt
¼ teaspoon pepper
⅛ teaspoon paprika
1 (3- to 3½-pound) broiler-fryer,
  quartered

Combine all ingredients except chicken, stirring well. Set sauce aside. Grill chicken, skin side down, over medium coals 50 to 60 minutes or until done, turning every 10 minutes. Baste chicken with sauce during last 20 minutes of grilling time. Yield: 4 servings.

PICNIC BARBECUED CHICKEN

2 cloves garlic, crushed
2 teaspoons butter or margarine,
  melted
1 cup catsup
¾ cup chili sauce
¼ cup firmly packed brown sugar
1 tablespoon celery seeds
1 tablespoon prepared mustard
2 tablespoons Worcestershire
  sauce
2 dashes of hot sauce
½ teaspoon salt
2 (2½- to 3-pound) broiler-fryers,
  quartered

Sauté garlic in melted butter in a small saucepan until tender. Stir in remaining ingredients except chicken; bring to a boil. Remove barbecue sauce from heat, and set aside.

Grill chicken, skin side up, over medium coals 15 minutes. Baste with reserved barbecue sauce. Grill an additional 40 minutes or until done. Baste every 10 minutes with remaining sauce. Yield: 8 servings.

HONEY-GLAZED CHICKEN

½ cup soy sauce
½ cup honey
1 teaspoon garlic powder
2 teaspoons dry mustard
1 teaspoon grated lemon rind
2 tablespoons lemon juice
½ teaspoon ground ginger
¼ teaspoon seasoned pepper
1 (3- to 3½-pound) broiler-fryer, cut up

Combine all ingredients except chicken, stirring well. Set sauce aside.

Grill chicken, skin side down, over medium coals 50 to 60 minutes or until done, turning every 10 minutes. Baste with sauce during last 20 minutes of grilling time. Yield: 4 servings.

SAVORY BARBECUED CHICKEN

1½ cups catsup
1⅓ cups pickle relish, drained
¼ cup firmly packed brown sugar
¼ cup soy sauce
2 tablespoons prepared mustard
¼ teaspoon pepper
2 cloves garlic, minced
2 (3- to 3½-pound) broiler-fryers, cut up

Combine all ingredients except chicken, stirring well. Set sauce aside.

Grill chicken, skin side down, over medium coals 1 hour or until done, turning every 10 minutes. Baste chicken with sauce during last 25 minutes of grilling time. Yield: 8 servings.

LEMONADE CHICKEN

1 (6-ounce) can frozen lemonade
    concentrate, thawed and undiluted
½ cup soy sauce
1 teaspoon seasoned salt
½ teaspoon celery salt
⅛ teaspoon garlic powder
2 (2½- to 3-pound) broiler-fryers,
    cut up

Combine all ingredients except chicken, stirring well. Set sauce aside.

Grill chicken over medium-hot coals 15 to 20 minutes, turning frequently. Baste with sauce. Grill chicken an additional 30 to 35 minutes or until done. Turn and baste frequently with remaining sauce. Yield: 8 servings.

DIXIE STUFFED CHICKEN BREASTS

8 chicken breast halves, boned and
    skinned
½ teaspoon seasoned salt
¼ teaspoon poultry seasoning
¼ teaspoon pepper
1 (4½-ounce) can deviled ham
1 cup soft breadcrumbs
2 teaspoons instant minced onion
½ cup butter or margarine
1 (0.7-ounce) envelope dry Parmesan
    salad dressing mix

Place each chicken breast half on a sheet of wax paper; flatten to ¼-inch thickness, using a meat mallet or rolling pin. Combine salt, poultry seasoning, and pepper, stirring well; sprinkle over chicken. Combine deviled ham, breadcrumbs, and onion, stirring well. Spread mixture evenly over chicken breast halves, and roll up, jellyroll fashion, starting with short sides. Secure with wooden picks. Combine remaining ingredients in a small saucepan. Cook, uncovered, over low heat until butter melts, stirring frequently. Remove sauce from heat.

Baste stuffed chicken breasts with sauce. Grill over medium coals 20 minutes, basting frequently. Turn chicken, and baste with remaining sauce. Grill an additional 20 minutes or until done. Yield: 8 servings.

GRILLED CHICKEN BREASTS

2 teaspoons Dijon mustard
4 chicken breast halves, skinned
¼ teaspoon freshly ground pepper
⅓ cup butter or margarine
1 teaspoon dried whole tarragon
2 teaspoons lemon juice
½ teaspoon garlic salt

Spread mustard on both sides of chicken, and sprinkle with pepper. Cover and refrigerate 2 to 4 hours.

Melt butter in a small saucepan over low heat; stir in remaining ingredients. Cook, uncovered, over low heat 5 minutes, stirring occasionally. Remove sauce from heat.

Baste chicken with sauce. Grill over medium coals 50 to 55 minutes or until done. Turn and baste every 10 minutes with remaining sauce. Yield: 4 servings.

FLAVORFUL BARBECUED CHICKEN

Hickory chips
2 cups vinegar
½ cup plus 2 tablespoons shortening
½ cup butter or margarine
3 tablespoons pepper
2 tablespoons red pepper
1 tablespoon plus 1½ teaspoons salt
8 chicken breast halves

Soak hickory chips in water to cover at least 1 hour. Drain.

Combine remaining ingredients except chicken in a medium saucepan; bring to a boil. Reduce heat, and simmer sauce,

uncovered, until shortening and butter melt. Remove sauce from heat.

Prepare fire in grill; let burn 15 to 20 minutes. Place wood chips over hot coals. Baste chicken with sauce, and grill over medium coals 45 to 55 minutes or until done. Turn and baste every 10 minutes with remaining sauce. Yield: 8 servings.

CHICKEN NAPOLI

1 cup butter or margarine
⅓ cup lime juice
2 (0.7-ounce) envelopes dry Italian salad dressing mix
8 chicken breast halves

Melt butter in a small saucepan over low heat; stir in lime juice and salad dressing mix. Remove sauce from heat.

Baste chicken with sauce, and grill skin side down over medium coals 40 minutes or until done. Turn and baste frequently with sauce. Yield: 8 servings.

GRILLED CHICKEN

8 chicken breast halves, skinned
2 cups soy sauce
1 cup vegetable oil
½ cup vinegar
¼ cup firmly packed brown sugar
1 tablespoon dried whole oregano
1 tablespoon dried whole thyme
2 teaspoons dry mustard

Place chicken in a large Dutch oven. Add water to cover; bring to a boil. Cover, reduce heat, and simmer 15 minutes. Drain chicken, and place in a large shallow container. Combine remaining ingredients, stirring well; pour marinade over chicken. Cover and refrigerate 4 hours, turning frequently.

Remove chicken from marinade. Grill over medium coals 10 minutes or until done, turning once. Yield: 8 servings.

RUMAKI KABOBS

2 large carrots, cut into ½-inch pieces
12 chicken livers (about 1 pound)
½ cup soy sauce
¼ cup firmly packed brown sugar
¼ teaspoon ground ginger
8 whole water chestnuts
12 slices bacon, cut in half
2 medium onions, quartered
1 large green pepper, cut into 1-inch
   pieces
Hot cooked rice

Cook carrots 1 minute in boiling water to cover. Drain and set aside.

Cut chicken livers in half. Dip each half into soy sauce. Combine remaining soy sauce, sugar, and ginger, stirring until sugar dissolves. Set chicken livers and soy sauce mixture aside.

Cut water chestnuts into thirds. Place a piece of water chestnut and a piece of chicken liver on each piece of bacon; roll up. Alternate chicken liver bundles and vegetables on skewers. Grill kabobs 15 to 20 minutes over medium coals or until chicken livers are done. Turn and baste frequently with soy sauce mixture. Serve over hot cooked rice. Yield: 4 servings.

SESAME CHICKEN KABOBS

2 whole chicken breasts, skinned,
   boned, and cut into 1-inch cubes
¼ cup soy sauce
¼ cup commercial Russian salad
   dressing
1 tablespoon sesame seeds
2 tablespoons lemon juice
¼ teaspoon garlic powder
¼ teaspoon ground ginger
1 green pepper, cut into 1-inch pieces
2 medium onions, cut into eighths
3 small zucchini, cut into ¾-inch pieces
1 pint cherry tomatoes

Place chicken cubes in a large shallow container. Combine soy sauce, dressing,

sesame seeds, juice, garlic powder, and ginger in a jar; cover tightly, and shake vigorously. Pour over chicken. Cover and refrigerate at least 2 hours, stirring chicken occasionally.

Remove chicken from marinade, reserving marinade. Alternate chicken and vegetables on skewers. Grill kabobs over medium-hot coals 15 to 20 minutes or until chicken is done. Turn and baste frequently with marinade. Yield: 6 servings.

HAWAIIAN KABOBS

1½ pounds boneless chicken breasts,
   cut into 1-inch cubes
1 (15¼-ounce) can unsweetened
   pineapple chunks, undrained
½ cup soy sauce
¼ cup vegetable oil
1 tablespoon brown sugar
1 teaspoon garlic powder
2 teaspoons ground ginger
1 teaspoon dry mustard
¼ teaspoon freshly ground pepper
1 large green pepper, cut into 1-inch
   pieces
12 medium-size fresh mushrooms
18 cherry tomatoes
Hot cooked rice

Place chicken cubes in a large shallow container. Drain pineapple, reserving ½ cup juice. Set pineapple chunks aside. Combine juice and next 7 ingredients in a small saucepan, stirring well; bring to a boil. Reduce heat, and simmer, uncovered, 5 minutes; pour over chicken. Cover and refrigerate at least 1 hour, stirring chicken occasionally.

Remove chicken from marinade, reserving marinade. Alternate chicken, pineapple, green pepper, mushrooms, and tomatoes on skewers. Grill kabobs over hot coals 20 minutes or until chicken is done. Turn and baste frequently with marinade. Serve over hot cooked rice. Yield: 6 servings.

Sauces

DRESSED-UP BARBECUE SAUCE

1 (18-ounce) bottle commercial
  barbecue sauce with onion bits
⅔ cup firmly packed brown sugar
½ cup Burgundy or other dry red wine
1 teaspoon Worcestershire sauce
Dash of hot sauce

Combine all ingredients, stirring well. Use sauce to baste chicken or lamb when grilling. Heat thoroughly to serve, if desired. Yield: 2½ cups.

PAPRIKA BARBECUE SAUCE

1 cup catsup
½ cup vinegar
½ cup butter or margarine
¼ cup firmly packed brown sugar
¼ cup paprika
Juice of 2 lemons
1 tablespoon pepper
1 tablespoon plus 1 teaspoon prepared
  horseradish
2 teaspoons prepared mustard
1 teaspoon Worcestershire sauce
¼ teaspoon hot sauce
1 clove garlic, minced

Combine all ingredients in a large saucepan, stirring well; bring to a boil. Reduce heat, and simmer sauce, uncovered, 10 to 15 minutes, stirring occasionally. Use sauce for basting, or serve with, chicken, beef, or ribs. Yield: 2 cups.

BOURBON BARBECUE SAUCE

1 cup catsup
⅓ cup bourbon
¼ cup vinegar
¼ cup molasses
2 cloves garlic, crushed
1 tablespoon Worcestershire sauce
1 tablespoon lemon juice
2 teaspoons soy sauce
½ teaspoon dry mustard
¼ teaspoon pepper

Combine all ingredients, stirring well. Use sauce to baste pork or beef when grilling. Yield: 2 cups.

WESTERN KENTUCKY-STYLE BARBECUE SAUCE

1¾ cups water
1 cup plus 2 tablespoons catsup
¼ cup plus 2 tablespoons
  Worcestershire sauce
1½ teaspoons red pepper
1 teaspoon paprika
1 teaspoon dry mustard
¾ teaspoon garlic salt
¾ teaspoon onion powder
¾ teaspoon pepper

Combine all ingredients in a saucepan. Cook, uncovered, over medium heat 20 minutes; stir occasionally. Use to baste chicken or ribs. Yield: about 3 cups.

LOW COUNTRY BARBECUE SAUCE

2 cups chopped tomatoes
1 medium onion, finely chopped
¼ cup butter or margarine, melted
¼ cup vinegar
1 tablespoon sugar
1 tablespoon paprika
1 tablespoon pepper
2 teaspoons salt
1½ teaspoons Worcestershire sauce
¼ teaspoon hot sauce
1 clove garlic
½ pod red pepper

Process tomatoes through a food mill. Set tomatoes aside.

Sauté onion in butter in a medium saucepan until tender. Stir in tomatoes and remaining ingredients; bring to a boil. Reduce heat, and simmer sauce, uncovered, 15 minutes, stirring occasionally. Remove and discard garlic and red pepper pod. Serve sauce over sliced pork. Yield: 2 cups.

FRESH TOMATO BARBECUE SAUCE

1 cup coarsely chopped onion
2 cloves garlic, minced
2 tablespoons butter or margarine, melted
5 small tomatoes, peeled and chopped
2 tablespoons Worcestershire sauce
2 tablespoons red wine vinegar
2 teaspoons salt
1 teaspoon chili powder
1 teaspoon dry mustard
½ cup dark corn syrup

Sauté onion and garlic in butter in a medium saucepan until tender. Stir in remaining ingredients except corn syrup; bring to a boil. Reduce heat, and simmer sauce, uncovered, 20 minutes, stirring occasionally. Stir in corn syrup, and simmer,

uncovered, an additional 10 minutes. Use sauce for basting, or serve with, beef or ribs. Yield: 3 cups.

1948 ORIGINAL BARBECUE SAUCE

1 medium onion, chopped
2 cloves garlic, minced
2 tablespoons butter or margarine, melted
1 (14½-ounce) can whole tomatoes
1 (8-ounce) can tomato sauce
½ cup chopped celery
⅓ cup vinegar
¼ cup chopped green pepper
2 fresh celery leaves, chopped
1 bay leaf
3 tablespoons molasses
1½ teaspoons salt
2 teaspoons dry mustard
2 teaspoons hot sauce
½ teaspoon ground cloves
½ teaspoon ground allspice
2 lemon slices

Sauté onion and garlic in butter in a saucepan until tender. Stir in remaining ingredients; bring to a boil. Reduce heat, and simmer, uncovered, 30 minutes; stir occasionally. Discard bay leaf and lemon slices. Process mixture through a food mill, if desired. Use sauce for basting, or serve with, chicken. Yield: 3 cups.

HAWAIIAN BARBECUE SAUCE

¾ cup unsweetened pineapple juice
½ cup vegetable oil
⅓ cup soy sauce
¼ cup lemon juice
¼ cup molasses
1 teaspoon ground ginger

Combine all ingredients, stirring well. Use sauce to baste chicken or lamb when grilling. Yield: 2 cups.

BARBECUE SAUCE FOR CHICKEN

2 cups butter or margarine
1 cup vinegar
½ (6-ounce) jar prepared mustard
¼ cup Worcestershire sauce

Melt butter in a medium saucepan over low heat. Stir in remaining ingredients; remove from heat. Cover and refrigerate sauce until ready to use. Heat thoroughly, and use to baste chicken when grilling. Yield: about 4 cups.

TEXAS BARBECUE SAUCE

2 cups butter or margarine, softened
2 tablespoons dry mustard
1 (5-ounce) bottle Worcestershire sauce
¼ cup garlic-flavored wine vinegar
3 tablespoons lemon juice
2 teaspoons hot sauce
Salt to taste
Red pepper to taste

Combine butter and mustard in a medium bowl, stirring until blended. Stir in remaining ingredients. Cover and refrigerate sauce 24 hours. Heat thoroughly, and use to baste beef, pork, or chicken when grilling. Yield: about 2½ cups.

EASY SWEET-AND-SOUR BARBECUE SAUCE

1 (12-ounce) jar orange marmalade
1 (12-ounce) bottle chili sauce
¼ cup vinegar
1 tablespoon Worcestershire sauce
1½ teaspoons celery seeds

Combine all ingredients; stir well. Use sauce for basting, or serve with, chicken, lamb, or ribs. Yield: about 3 cups.

PEANUT BUTTER BARBECUE SAUCE

¼ cup butter or margarine
½ cup vinegar
Juice of 1 lime
1 tablespoon creamy peanut butter
1 teaspoon salt
1 teaspoon pepper
1 teaspoon celery seeds

Melt butter in a small saucepan over low heat. Stir in remaining ingredients; bring to a boil. Reduce heat, and simmer sauce, uncovered, 20 minutes, stirring occasionally. Use sauce for basting, or serve with, chicken. Yield: about ½ cup.

TENNESSEE BASTING SAUCE

3 cups vinegar
1 cup Worcestershire sauce
¼ cup dry mustard
¼ cup catsup
¼ cup butter or margarine
1 medium onion, quartered
1 lemon, quartered
16 whole cloves
10 bay leaves
5 cloves garlic
1 tablespoon salt
1 teaspoon dried whole oregano
1 teaspoon dried whole rosemary
½ teaspoon pepper
¼ teaspoon red pepper
¼ teaspoon hot sauce

Combine all ingredients in a small Dutch oven; bring to a boil. Reduce heat, and simmer sauce, uncovered, 15 minutes, stirring occasionally. Strain sauce, discarding onion, lemon, cloves, bay leaves, and garlic. Use to baste pork when grilling. Yield: about 4 cups.

HORSERADISH BARBECUE SAUCE

1 medium onion, chopped
1 cup water
1 cup catsup
½ cup vinegar
1 tablespoon chopped fresh parsley
1 tablespoon brown sugar
1 tablespoon prepared horseradish
1 tablespoon prepared mustard
1 teaspoon pepper

Combine all ingredients in a medium saucepan, stirring well; bring to a boil. Reduce heat, and simmer sauce, uncovered, 10 to 15 minutes, stirring occasionally. Serve horseradish sauce with pork or beef roasts. Yield: 3 cups.

CREOLE BARBECUE SAUCE

2 cups water
2 cups vinegar
½ cup butter or margarine
¼ cup sugar
¼ cup Worcestershire sauce
¼ cup catsup
2 drops of hot sauce
1 large red onion, chopped
6 stalks celery, chopped
1 lemon, thinly sliced
1 bay leaf
1 tablespoon salt
2 tablespoons red pepper
2 tablespoons celery seeds
1 teaspoon garlic salt
1 teaspoon dry mustard
1 teaspoon pepper

Combine all ingredients in a large Dutch oven, stirring well; bring to a boil. Reduce heat, and simmer sauce, uncovered, 30 minutes, stirring occasionally. Remove and discard bay leaf. Use sauce for basting, or serve with, beef, pork, or chicken. Yield: about 7 cups.

QUICK-AND-EASY BEER BARBECUE SAUCE

1½ cups chili sauce
1 cup beer
2 tablespoons grated onion
2 tablespoons vinegar
2 tablespoons Worcestershire sauce
2 teaspoons sugar
2 teaspoons chili powder

Combine all ingredients in a medium saucepan, stirring well; bring mixture to a boil. Reduce heat, and simmer sauce, uncovered, 2 minutes, stirring frequently. Use sauce to baste beef, chicken, frankfurters, or ribs when grilling. Yield: about 2½ cups.

MUSTARD BARBECUE SAUCE

2 cups prepared mustard
1 cup mayonnaise
½ cup water
¼ cup plus 2 tablespoons catsup
¼ cup butter or margarine
2 tablespoons sugar
2 tablespoons Worcestershire sauce
1 teaspoon browning-and-seasoning sauce
½ teaspoon salt
½ teaspoon seasoned salt
¼ teaspoon pepper
¼ teaspoon liquid smoke

Combine all ingredients in a small Dutch oven, stirring well; bring to a boil. Reduce heat, and simmer, uncovered, 10 minutes; stir occasionally. Use sauce for basting, or serve with, chicken, lamb, pork, or ribs. Yield: about 4 cups.

Accompaniments

Salads

SIMPLY GOOD SALAD

2 cups torn spinach
2 cups torn iceberg lettuce
1 cup (4 ounces) shredded sharp
  Cheddar cheese
1 hard-cooked egg, chopped
1 small green onion, chopped
1 (8-ounce) can unsweetened pineapple
  tidbits, drained
Commercial buttermilk-style salad
  dressing, chilled

Combine spinach, lettuce, cheese, egg, green onion, and pineapple in a large salad bowl; toss gently. Serve with salad dressing. Yield: 6 servings.

MARINATED TOMATO SLICES

4 tomatoes, sliced
1 onion, thinly sliced
1 cup vegetable oil
⅓ cup red wine vinegar
⅛ teaspoon garlic powder
Salt and pepper to taste
Lettuce leaves (optional)

Arrange tomato and onion slices in a large shallow container. Combine oil, vinegar, and garlic powder, stirring well; pour over tomato and onion. Sprinkle with salt and pepper. Cover and refrigerate at least 1 hour. Serve over lettuce leaves, if desired. Yield: 6 servings.

MEDITERRANEAN SPRING SALAD

½ pound small new potatoes
½ cup olive oil
2 tablespoons lemon juice
1 clove garlic, crushed
2 teaspoons dried whole oregano
¼ teaspoon salt
6 cups torn mixed salad greens
2 small tomatoes, cut into wedges
1 small red onion, thinly sliced and
  separated into rings
1 small cucumber, thinly sliced
½ cup crumbled feta cheese

Scrub potatoes. Cook in boiling salted water to cover 20 minutes or until tender; drain well, and cool. Peel and thinly slice potatoes; place in a shallow container. Combine oil, juice, garlic, oregano, and salt, stirring well; pour over potatoes. Cover and refrigerate 1 hour. Drain potatoes, reserving marinade.

Place salad greens in a large salad bowl. Arrange potatoes, tomatoes, onion, cucumber, and cheese over top. Serve with marinade. Yield: 8 servings.

SEVEN-LAYER SALAD

1 small head lettuce, coarsely chopped
  or shredded
1½ cups chopped celery
1½ cups chopped green pepper
1½ cups chopped red onion
3 (8½-ounce) cans small English peas,
  drained
2¼ cups mayonnaise
2 teaspoons sugar
Grated Parmesan cheese
6 slices bacon, cooked and crumbled

Layer lettuce, celery, green pepper, onion, and peas in a large salad bowl; spread mayonnaise evenly over top. Sprinkle with remaining ingredients. Cover tightly, and refrigerate at least 8 hours. Yield: 6 servings.

BOSTON TOSSED SALAD

½ cup olive oil
¼ cup corn oil
¼ cup red wine vinegar
½ teaspoon lemon-pepper seasoning
¼ teaspoon chopped fresh parsley
1 head Boston lettuce, torn
1 (11-ounce) can mandarin oranges,
  drained
½ small red onion, thinly sliced and
  separated into rings
12 large fresh mushrooms, sliced

Combine first 5 ingredients in a jar. Cover tightly, and shake vigorously. Refrigerate dressing mixture several hours.
Combine lettuce, oranges, onion, and mushrooms in a salad bowl, tossing gently. Serve with dressing mixture. Yield: 6 servings.

SPINACH SALAD

½ cup vegetable oil
¼ cup sugar
¼ cup chili sauce
1 small onion, minced
2 tablespoons red wine vinegar
½ teaspoon salt
½ teaspoon dry mustard
½ teaspoon Worcestershire sauce
¼ teaspoon red pepper
1 pound spinach, torn
⅔ cup torn Bibb lettuce
1 hard-cooked egg, grated
¾ cup cooked and crumbled bacon

Combine first 9 ingredients in a jar. Cover tightly, and shake vigorously. Refrigerate dressing mixture several hours.
Combine spinach and lettuce in a salad bowl. Sprinkle egg and bacon over top of salad. Serve with chilled dressing mixture. Yield: 4 servings.

CRISPY COLESLAW

1 medium cabbage, shredded
1 small onion, minced
½ cup sweet pickle cubes
1 cup mayonnaise
¼ cup sugar
¼ cup vinegar
1 tablespoon salt
1 teaspoon dillseeds
1 teaspoon celery seeds or celery salt
¼ teaspoon pepper
Leaf lettuce (optional)
Green pepper rings (optional)
Pimiento strips (optional)

Combine first 3 ingredients in a large bowl. Set cabbage mixture aside.
Combine mayonnaise, sugar, vinegar, and seasonings; stir well. Pour dressing mixture over cabbage mixture; toss well. Cover and refrigerate several hours. Serve coleslaw in a lettuce-lined bowl, and garnish with green pepper and pimiento, if desired. Yield: 12 servings.

COUNTRY-STYLE COLESLAW

1 large cabbage, coarsely chopped
1½ cups shredded carrots
1 cup chopped green pepper
¼ cup chopped green onions
1 cup mayonnaise
3 tablespoons sugar
3 tablespoons vinegar
1½ teaspoons salt
¾ teaspoon dry mustard
¼ teaspoon celery seeds
1 small green pepper, sliced into rings
(optional)

Combine first 4 ingredients in a large bowl. Set cabbage mixture aside.

Combine mayonnaise, sugar, vinegar, salt, mustard, and celery seeds, stirring well; pour over cabbage mixture, and toss well. Cover and refrigerate until chilled. Garnish with green pepper rings, if desired. Yield: 12 servings.

GERMAN POTATO SALAD

4 medium potatoes
8 slices bacon
⅓ cup water
⅓ cup vinegar
¼ cup sugar
2 tablespoons all-purpose flour
1 small green pepper, chopped
1 small onion, chopped
¼ cup chopped celery
1 tablespoon chopped pimiento

Scrub potatoes. Cook in boiling water to cover for 20 minutes or until tender. Drain and cool slightly. Peel potatoes; cut into ½-inch cubes, and set aside.

Cook bacon in a large skillet until crisp; remove bacon, reserving ¼ cup drippings in skillet. Crumble bacon, and set aside. Add water, vinegar, sugar, and flour to drippings in skillet, stirring well. Cook over medium heat until slightly thickened. Remove vinegar mixture from heat, and set aside.

Combine potatoes, green pepper, onion, celery, and pimiento in a large bowl. Top with vinegar mixture, and toss gently. Yield: 6 servings.

SOUR CREAM POTATO SALAD

6 to 8 medium potatoes
2 tablespoons sweet pickle relish
2 tablespoons finely chopped onion
2 tablespoons chopped fresh parsley
1 (2-ounce) jar chopped pimiento, drained
2 tablespoons vinegar
1 tablespoon prepared mustard
1 teaspoon salt
Pepper to taste
1 (8-ounce) carton commercial sour cream
1½ cups chopped celery
2 hard-cooked eggs, chopped

Scrub potatoes. Cook in boiling water to cover for 30 minutes or until tender. Drain and cool. Peel potatoes; cut into ½-inch cubes, and set aside.

Combine relish, onion, parsley, pimiento, vinegar, mustard, salt, and pepper in a large salad bowl, stirring well; fold in sour cream. Add potatoes, celery, and eggs; toss gently. Cover and refrigerate at least 1 hour. Yield: 8 servings.

Vegetables

ALMOND ASPARAGUS

2½ pounds fresh asparagus spears
¼ cup plus 1 tablespoon butter or
   margarine
1¼ cups slivered almonds, toasted
2 tablespoons plus 1½ teaspoons
   lemon juice
¼ teaspoon salt
⅛ teaspoon pepper

Snap off tough ends of asparagus. Remove scales from stalks with a knife or vegetable peeler, if desired.

Melt butter in a large skillet; add asparagus, and sauté 3 to 4 minutes. Cover skillet, and simmer an additional 2 minutes or until asparagus is crisp-tender. Add remaining ingredients; toss gently. Yield: 10 servings.

HERB-SEASONED GREEN BEANS

1½ pounds fresh green beans
¾ teaspoon salt
¾ cup chopped onion
¼ cup plus 2 tablespoons chopped
   celery
1 large clove garlic, minced
3 tablespoons butter or margarine
¾ teaspoon dried whole rosemary,
   crushed
¾ teaspoon dried whole basil

Remove strings from beans; cut beans into 1-inch pieces. Wash beans thoroughly in cold water.

Place beans, salt, and about 1½ cups water in a large saucepan; bring to a boil. Cover, reduce heat, and simmer 10 minutes. Stir in remaining ingredients; cover and cook an additional 10 to 15 minutes or until tender. Yield: 6 servings.

FRESH GREEN BEANS

1½ pounds fresh green beans
About 6 cups water
⅓ pound diced salt pork or ham hock
Salt to taste
⅛ teaspoon sugar

Remove strings from beans; cut beans into 1½-inch pieces. Wash beans thoroughly in cold water; set aside.

Place water in a large saucepan, and add salt pork; bring to a boil. Cover, reduce heat, and simmer about 5 minutes. Stir in beans and remaining ingredients. Cover and simmer an additional 25 to 35 minutes or until beans are tender. Yield: 6 servings.

BARBECUED PINTO BEANS

1 (16-ounce) package dried pinto beans
2 slices bacon, diced
1½ teaspoons salt
1½ cups commercial barbecue sauce or
   see Sauce chapter

Sort and wash beans; place in a large Dutch oven. Cover with water 2 inches above beans; let soak at least 8 hours. Drain beans well.

Combine beans, bacon, and salt in Dutch oven. Cover with water 3 inches above beans; bring to a boil. Cover, reduce heat, and simmer 2½ hours or until beans are tender. Drain. Stir in barbecue sauce. Simmer, uncovered, an additional 30 minutes or until desired consistency, stirring occasionally. Yield: 8 servings.

CORN-ON-THE-COB WITH HERB BUTTER

½ cup butter or margarine, softened
2 tablespoons chopped fresh parsley
2 tablespoons chopped fresh chives
½ teaspoon dried salad herbs
8 ears fresh corn
About 1 gallon water

Combine first 4 ingredients, stirring well. Set butter mixture aside.

Remove husks and silks from corn just before cooking. Bring water to a boil in a large Dutch oven, and add corn. Return to a boil, and boil 8 to 10 minutes. Drain well. Spread butter mixture over hot corn. Yield: 8 servings.

CORN PUDDING

2 cups fresh corn cut from cob
¼ cup all-purpose flour
2 to 3 tablespoons sugar
1 teaspoon salt
2 cups milk
2 eggs, beaten
2 tablespoons butter or margarine, melted

Combine corn, flour, sugar, and salt in a large bowl, stirring well. Combine remaining ingredients, stirring well; add to corn mixture.

Pour corn mixture into a lightly greased 1½-quart casserole. Bake at 350° for 1 hour, stirring twice during first 30 minutes. Yield: 6 servings.

MINTED PEAS

2½ pounds fresh English peas
2 tablespoons jellied mint sauce
1 tablespoon butter or margarine
½ teaspoon salt
¼ teaspoon pepper

Shell and rinse peas. Combine peas and boiling water to cover in a large saucepan.

Boil 10 to 12 minutes or until peas are tender. Drain peas, reserving ¼ cup cooking liquid.

Return peas and reserved liquid to saucepan; stir in remaining ingredients. Cook over medium heat 2 to 3 minutes or until mint sauce melts, stirring constantly. Yield: 4 servings.

PARSLEY NEW POTATOES

1½ pounds small new potatoes
2½ cups water
Salt to taste
¼ cup plus 2 tablespoons butter or margarine, melted
3 tablespoons chopped fresh parsley

Wash potatoes; peel a strip around center of each potato, if desired.

Combine potatoes, water, and salt in a large saucepan; bring to a boil. Cover, reduce heat, and cook 15 minutes or until potatoes are tender. Drain well; transfer potatoes to a serving bowl.

Combine butter and parsley, stirring well. Spoon butter mixture over hot potatoes. Yield: 4 servings.

CHARCOAL-BAKED POTATOES

6 medium-size baking potatoes, unpeeled
Butter or sour cream
Salt and pepper to taste

Wrap each potato securely in heavy-duty aluminum foil. Place foil-wrapped potatoes around gray coals on bottom of grill. Cook 1 hour and 15 minutes or until done. Turn potatoes every 20 minutes, using hot pads or tongs.

Unwrap potatoes, and cut a slit in top of each. Press sides to loosen inside of each potato. Add butter or sour cream, and sprinkle with salt and pepper to taste. Serve hot. Yield: 6 servings.

HERBED POTATOES ON THE GRILL

¼ cup finely chopped celery
¾ cup butter or margarine, melted
1 teaspoon dried whole oregano
½ teaspoon salt
¼ teaspoon garlic powder
⅛ teaspoon pepper
6 medium-size baking potatoes, unpeeled
1 medium onion, thinly sliced

Sauté celery in butter in a small saucepan until tender. Stir in oregano, salt, garlic powder, and pepper. Remove butter mixture from heat, and keep warm.

Wash potatoes; cut each into ½-inch slices, cutting to, but not through, bottom peel. Place a slice of onion between each slice of potato. Place each potato on a square of heavy-duty aluminum foil; drizzle about 2 tablespoons butter mixture over each. Fold foil edges over, and wrap securely. Grill foil-wrapped potatoes over medium coals 1 hour or until done. Yield: 6 servings.

ZIPPY ZUCCHINI SKILLET

2 tablespoons vegetable oil
4 medium zucchini, thinly sliced
1 medium onion, chopped
1 (16-ounce) can whole kernel corn, drained
1 (4-ounce) can chopped green chiles
2 teaspoons seeded chopped jalapeño peppers
¼ teaspoon salt
⅛ teaspoon garlic powder
½ cup (2 ounces) shredded Cheddar cheese

Heat oil in a large skillet; add zucchini and onion, and sauté 10 minutes or until tender. Stir in remaining ingredients except cheese; cook, stirring occasionally, until thoroughly heated. Remove from heat; stir in cheese. Yield: 6 servings.

CHEESY STUFFED SQUASH

6 medium-size yellow squash
½ pound bacon
1 small onion, chopped
¾ cup soft breadcrumbs
1 cup (4 ounces) shredded sharp Cheddar cheese
Paprika
Fresh parsley sprigs (optional)

Wash squash thoroughly, and cook in boiling salted water to cover for 8 to 10 minutes or until tender but still firm. Drain squash and cool slightly. Remove and discard stems. Cut each squash in half lengthwise; remove and reserve pulp, leaving a firm shell.

Cook bacon in a large skillet until crisp; drain well, reserving 2 tablespoons bacon drippings in skillet. Crumble bacon, and set aside. Sauté onion in bacon drippings until tender; stir in crumbled bacon, breadcrumbs, and squash pulp.

Place squash shells in a 13- x 9- x 2-inch baking dish. Spoon squash mixture into shells, and top with cheese. Broil 6 inches from heat about 5 minutes or just until cheese is melted. Sprinkle with paprika, and garnish with parsley, if desired. Yield: 6 servings.

EASY SUCCOTASH

2 cups fresh lima beans (about 1 pound)
4 cups fresh corn cut from cob (about 8 ears)
½ cup whipping cream
3 tablespoons butter or margarine
½ teaspoon salt
⅛ teaspoon pepper

Cook beans in boiling salted water to cover for 15 minutes or until almost tender; drain. Add remaining ingredients; stir well. Cook, uncovered, over low heat 8 to 10 minutes or until corn is done; stir frequently. Yield: 6 servings.

SUMMER GARDEN MEDLEY

2 tablespoons chopped onion
1 tablespoon butter or margarine,
   melted
1 cup fresh corn cut from cob
2 small tomatoes, peeled and cubed
2 small yellow squash, sliced
½ teaspoon salt
¼ teaspoon sugar
¼ teaspoon dried whole oregano
⅛ teaspoon pepper

Sauté onion in butter in a small Dutch oven until tender. Add remaining ingredients, stirring well. Cover and cook over medium heat 15 minutes or until all vegetables are tender. Yield: 4 servings.

VEGETABLES IN A PACKET

3 medium tomatoes, quartered
3 medium-size yellow squash,
   sliced
1 small onion, sliced
1 teaspoon minced fresh basil
½ teaspoon salt
⅛ teaspoon pepper
2 teaspoons butter or margarine

Place tomatoes, squash, and onion on a large piece of heavy-duty aluminum foil; sprinkle with basil, salt, and pepper. Dot with butter. Fold foil edges over, and wrap securely. Grill packet over medium coals 20 to 25 minutes, turning after 10 minutes. Yield: 4 servings.

Breads

MEXICAN CORNBREAD

1 tablespoon vegetable oil
1½ cups self-rising cornmeal
1 cup buttermilk
2 eggs, beaten
3 tablespoons vegetable oil
1 (8¾-ounce) can cream-style corn
½ cup chopped green pepper
6 slices bacon, cooked and crumbled
¼ cup chopped canned jalapeño
   peppers
Dash of garlic powder
2 cups (8 ounces) shredded sharp
   Cheddar cheese, divided

Grease a 10½-inch cast-iron skillet with 1 tablespoon oil. Heat at 350° for 10 minutes or until very hot.
Combine remaining ingredients except cheese in a medium bowl, stirring well. Pour half of cornmeal mixture into skillet.

Sprinkle with 1 cup cheese. Top with remaining cornmeal mixture. Bake at 350° for 45 minutes. Sprinkle with remaining 1 cup cheese, and bake an additional 10 minutes. Yield: 12 servings.

CORN MUFFINS

1½ cups biscuit mix
½ cup cornmeal
2 tablespoons sugar
2 eggs, beaten
⅔ cup milk

Combine first 3 ingredients in a large bowl; make a well in center of mixture. Combine eggs and milk; add to dry ingredients, stirring just until moistened. Spoon into greased muffin pans. Bake at 400° for 20 minutes or until golden brown. Yield: about 1 dozen.

NANNIE'S BISCUITS

⅔ **cup shortening**
1½ **cups self-rising flour**
⅔ **cup buttermilk**

Cut shortening into flour with a pastry blender until mixture resembles coarse meal. Add buttermilk, stirring with a fork until dry ingredients are moistened. Turn dough out onto a lightly floured surface, and lightly knead 4 or 5 times.

Roll dough out to ½-inch thickness, and cut with a 1½-inch biscuit cutter. Place biscuits on a lightly greased baking sheet; bake at 425° for 12 minutes or until golden brown. Yield: 3½ dozen.

GRILLED GARLIC BREAD

1 **tablespoon plus 1½ teaspoons butter**
  or margarine, softened
½ **teaspoon garlic powder**
½ **(8-ounce) loaf French bread**

Combine butter and garlic powder in a small bowl, stirring until blended. Cut French bread into 8 slices, and spread each slice with butter mixture.

Grill bread slices over medium coals 2 minutes or until golden brown. Turn bread slices, and grill an additional 2 minutes or until golden brown. Serve hot. Yield: 4 servings.

EASY GARLIC ROLLS

1 **(1-pound) loaf frozen commercial**
  bread dough, thawed
¼ **cup butter or margarine, melted**
1 **egg, beaten**
1 **tablespoon chopped fresh parsley**
½ **teaspoon garlic salt**

Divide dough into 20 portions; shape each portion into a ball. Combine remaining ingredients, stirring well. Dip dough balls into butter mixture, and place in a lightly greased 9-inch round cakepan. Cover and let rise in a warm place (85°), free from drafts, 1 hour or until doubled in bulk. Bake at 350° for 25 to 30 minutes or until golden brown. Yield: 20 rolls.

Desserts

BRANDY-CHOCOLATE MOUSSE

1 **(6-ounce) package semisweet**
  chocolate morsels
¼ **cup plus 1 tablespoon butter**
4 **eggs, separated**
2 **tablespoons brandy**
¼ **cup sifted powdered sugar**
Whipped cream (optional)

Place chocolate and butter in top of a double boiler; bring water to a boil. Reduce heat to low; cook until melted. Remove from heat; stir in egg yolks, one at a time, beating well with a wooden spoon after each addition. Cool. Stir in brandy and sugar, beating well. Set aside.

Beat egg whites (at room temperature) until stiff but not dry; gently fold egg whites into chocolate mixture. Spoon mousse into stemmed glasses. Cover and refrigerate until serving time. Garnish each serving with whipped cream, if desired. Yield: 6 servings.

BAKED CUSTARD

2 eggs, beaten
2 tablespoons sugar
⅛ teaspoon salt
Dash of ground nutmeg
1 teaspoon vanilla extract
1½ cups milk, scalded
Sliced fresh strawberries
Fresh blueberries

Combine first 5 ingredients; stir until blended. Gradually add scalded milk; stir constantly. Pour mixture into four 6-ounce custard cups. Set custard cups in a 9-inch square baking pan; pour hot water into pan to a depth of 1 inch.

Bake at 350° for 30 minutes or until a knife inserted in center comes out clean. Remove custard cups from water; cool. Refrigerate until chilled. Top with fresh fruit before serving. Yield: 4 servings.

CHERRY CORDIAL DESSERT

½ gallon vanilla ice cream,
    softened
4 (1.45-ounce) milk chocolate
    candy bars, finely chopped
1 cup maraschino cherries,
    halved
½ cup coarsely chopped pecans
Sweetened whipped cream
Grated semisweet chocolate
Maraschino cherries
¼ cup créme de cacao, divided

Gently combine first 4 ingredients; spoon into a 9-inch springform pan. Cover and freeze until firm.

Place dessert on a serving platter, and remove rim from springform pan. Garnish with whipped cream, grated chocolate, and maraschino cherries. To serve, spoon about 1 teaspoon créme de cacao over each slice. Serve immediately. Yield: one 9-inch dessert.

DELUXE BLUEBERRY CHEESECAKE

1½ cups graham cracker crumbs
2 tablespoons sugar
¼ cup plus 2 tablespoons butter or
    margarine, melted
1½ teaspoons ground cinnamon
3 (8-ounce) packages cream cheese,
    softened
1 cup sugar
3 eggs
1 teaspoon vanilla extract, divided
1 (16-ounce) carton commercial sour
    cream
3 tablespoons sugar
1 (21-ounce) can blueberry pie filling

Combine first 4 ingredients in a medium bowl; mix well. Press into a 10-inch springform pan; set aside.

Beat cream cheese in a large bowl until light. Gradually add 1 cup sugar, beating until fluffy. Add eggs, one at a time, beating well after each addition. Stir in ½ teaspoon vanilla. Pour cream cheese mixture into prepared pan; bake at 375° for 25 to 35 minutes or until cheesecake is set.

Beat sour cream in a small bowl at medium speed of an electric mixer for 2 minutes. Add 3 tablespoons sugar and remaining ½ teaspoon vanilla; beat 1 minute. Spread over cheesecake.

Bake cheesecake at 500° for 5 to 8 minutes or until bubbly. Remove from oven, and cool. Gently spread pie filling over top. Cover and refrigerate at least 8 hours. Place cheesecake on a serving platter, and remove rim from springform pan before serving. Yield: 10 servings.

CREAM CHEESE POUND CAKE

1½ cups chopped pecans, divided
1½ cups butter or margarine, softened
1 (8-ounce) package cream cheese, softened
3 cups sugar
6 eggs
3 cups sifted cake flour
Dash of salt
1½ teaspoons vanilla extract

Sprinkle ½ cup pecans in a greased and floured 10-inch tube pan. Set aside.

Cream butter and cream cheese in a large bowl. Gradually add sugar; beat well. Add eggs, one at a time, beating well after each addition. Add flour and salt, stirring until combined. Stir in vanilla and remaining 1 cup pecans.

Pour batter into prepared pan. Bake at 325° for 1½ hours or until a wooden pick inserted in center comes out clean. Cool in pan 10 minutes; remove from pan, and cool completely on a wire rack. Yield: one 10-inch cake.

COTTONWOOD CARROT CAKE

2 cups sifted cake flour
2 teaspoons baking soda
2 teaspoons ground cinnamon
2 teaspoons ground allspice
½ teaspoon salt
1⅓ cups vegetable oil
4 eggs, well beaten
2 cups sugar
3 cups grated carrots
Frosting (recipe follows)

Combine first 5 ingredients, stirring well. Set dry ingredients aside.

Combine oil, eggs, and sugar in a large bowl; beat at medium speed of an electric mixer until blended. Add dry ingredients, beating well. Stir in carrots.

Pour batter into a greased and floured 13- x 9- x 2-inch baking pan. Bake at 325° for 55 minutes or until a wooden pick inserted in center comes out clean. Cool completely, and spread frosting over top of cake. Yield: one 13- x 9-inch cake.

Frosting:

1 (8-ounce) package cream cheese, softened
½ cup butter or margarine, softened
1 (16-ounce) package powdered sugar, sifted
½ cup raisins, chopped
½ cup flaked coconut
½ cup chopped pecans
1 teaspoon vanilla extract

Combine cream cheese and butter in a medium bowl; cream well. Gradually add sugar; beat well. Add remaining ingredients; beat at high speed of an electric mixer until spreading consistency. Yield: frosting for one 13- x 9-inch cake.

CHOCOLATE FUDGE CAKE

½ cup butter or margarine, softened
1 (16-ounce) package brown sugar
3 eggs
3 (1-ounce) squares unsweetened chocolate, melted and cooled
2¼ cups sifted cake flour
2 teaspoons baking soda
½ teaspoon salt
1 (8-ounce) carton commercial sour cream
1 cup hot water
1½ teaspoons vanilla extract
Frosting (recipe follows)
Toasted pecan halves (optional)

Cream butter; gradually add brown sugar, beating well. Add eggs, one at a time, beating well after each addition. Add chocolate, mixing well.

Combine flour, soda, and salt; gradually add to chocolate mixture alternately with sour cream; beat well after each addition. Add water and vanilla; stir well.

Pour batter into 3 greased and floured 9-inch cakepans. Bake at 350° for 25 minutes or until a wooden pick inserted in center comes out clean. Let cool in pans 10 minutes. Remove from pans; place on wire racks to cool completely.

Spread frosting between layers and on top and sides of cake. Garnish top of cake with toasted pecan halves, if desired. Yield: one 9-inch layer cake.

Frosting:

**4 (1-ounce) squares unsweetened
  chocolate
⅓ cup butter or margarine
1 (16-ounce) package powdered sugar
½ cup milk
2 teaspoons vanilla extract**

Combine chocolate and butter in a large saucepan; cook over low heat until melted, stirring constantly. Remove chocolate mixture from heat, and cool.

Sift sugar; add to cooled chocolate mixture alternately with remaining ingredients. Beat at high speed of an electric mixer until spreading consistency. Yield: frosting for one 9-inch layer cake.

CRÈME DE MENTHE BROWNIES

**½ cup butter or margarine, softened
1 cup sugar
4 eggs
1 cup all-purpose flour
½ teaspoon salt
1 (16-ounce) can chocolate syrup
1 teaspoon vanilla extract
¼ cup butter or margarine, softened
2 cups sifted powdered sugar
2 tablespoons creme de menthe
1 (6-ounce) package semisweet
  chocolate morsels
¼ cup butter or margarine**

Cream ½ cup butter in a medium bowl; gradually add 1 cup sugar, beating until light and fluffy. Add eggs, one at a time, beating well after each addition.

Combine flour and salt; add to creamed mixture alternately with chocolate syrup, beginning and ending with flour mixture. Stir in vanilla.

Pour batter into a greased and floured 13- x 9- x 2-inch baking pan. Bake at 350° for 25 to 30 minutes. Cool completely (brownies will shrink from sides of pan while cooling).

Cream ¼ cup butter in a small bowl; gradually add 2 cups powdered sugar and crème de menthe, mixing well. Spread evenly over brownies; cover and refrigerate about 1 hour.

Combine morsels and ¼ cup butter in top of a double boiler; bring water to a boil. Reduce heat to low; cook until chocolate and butter melt. Spread over brownies; cover and refrigerate at least 1 hour. Cut into squares. Yield: 3½ dozen.

S'MORES

**6 (1.45-ounce) milk chocolate candy
  bars, broken in half crosswise
12 graham crackers, broken in half
  crosswise
12 large marshmallows**

Place chocolate bar halves on top of 12 graham cracker halves. Toast marshmallows over an open fire. Place toasted marshmallows on top of chocolate, and cover with remaining graham cracker halves to form a sandwich. Press to seal. Serve immediately. Yield: 12 servings.

LEMON MERINGUE PIE

1½ cups sugar
⅓ cup cornstarch
¼ teaspoon salt
1½ cups cold water
½ cup lemon juice
5 eggs, separated
2 tablespoons butter or margarine
1 to 2 teaspoons grated lemon rind
1 baked 9-inch pastry shell
¼ teaspoon cream of tartar
½ cup plus 2 tablespoons sugar
½ teaspoon vanilla extract

Combine first 3 ingredients in a large saucepan, stirring well. Gradually add water and lemon juice, stirring until mixture is smooth.

Beat egg yolks until thick and lemon colored; gradually stir into lemon mixture. Add butter. Cook over medium heat, stirring constantly, until thickened and bubbly. Cook mixture an additional minute, stirring constantly. Remove from heat, and stir in grated lemon rind. Pour into baked pastry shell.

Combine egg whites (at room temperature) and cream of tartar in a large bowl; beat until foamy. Gradually add ½ cup plus 2 tablespoons sugar, 1 tablespoon at a time, beating until stiff peaks form. Beat in vanilla. Spread meringue over filling, sealing to edge of pastry. Bake at 350° for 12 to 15 minutes or until meringue is golden brown. Cool to room temperature. Yield: one 9-inch pie.

OLD-FASHIONED PEACH COBBLER

4 cups sliced fresh peaches
1 cup sugar
½ cup butter or margarine
1½ cups all-purpose flour
¾ teaspoon salt
½ cup shortening
¼ cup plus 1 tablespoon cold water

Combine sliced peaches, sugar, and butter in a medium saucepan; bring to a boil. Reduce heat, and simmer, uncovered, until peaches are tender and mixture thickens. Pour peach mixture into a lightly buttered 10- x 6- x 2-inch baking dish, and set aside.

Combine flour and salt in a small bowl; cut in shortening with a pastry blender until mixture resembles coarse meal. Sprinkle water evenly over flour mixture, and stir with a fork until all ingredients are moistened. Shape pastry into a ball.

Roll pastry out to ⅛-inch thickness on a lightly floured surface; cut into 1-inch strips. Arrange half of strips in lattice design over peaches. Bake at 350° for 35 minutes. Remove from oven, and gently press baked pastry into peach mixture. Repeat lattice design over peaches with remaining pastry strips. Return cobbler to oven, and bake an additional 40 minutes. Yield: 6 servings.

CINNAMON-BAKED APPLES

6 large baking apples, peeled and cored
¼ cup plus 2 tablespoons sugar, divided
1½ teaspoons ground cinnamon, divided
1½ teaspoons ground nutmeg, divided
2 tablespoons butter or margarine, divided
½ to ¾ cup apple juice
Red food coloring (optional)

Place apples in a shallow 2-quart casserole; pour 1 tablespoon sugar into cavity of each apple. Sprinkle each with ¼ teaspoon cinnamon and ¼ teaspoon nutmeg; top with 1 teaspoon butter.

Place apple juice in a saucepan, and bring to a boil; stir in food coloring, if desired. Pour mixture into casserole. Bake, uncovered, at 400° for 50 to 60 minutes or until tender; baste occasionally with juice mixture. Yield: 6 servings.

Menus

PICNIC ON THE GROUNDS
(serves 8)

Mediterranean Spring Salad (page 43)
Picnic Barbecued Chicken (page 35)
Corn-on-the-Cob with
Herb Butter (page 47)
Commercial Italian Bread
Chocolate Fudge Cake (page 52)

A MEAT AND POTATOES SUPPER
(serves 6)

Seven-Layer Salad (page 44)
Grilled Black Pepper Steak (page 8)
Herbed Potatoes on the Grill (page 48)
Cheesy Stuffed Squash (page 48)
Corn Muffins (page 49)
Orange Sherbet

BEEF 'N' BISCUITS
(serves 6)

German Potato Salad (page 45)
Saucy Stove-Top Barbecue (page 5)
Fresh Broccoli Spears
Nannie's Biscuits (page 50)
Vanilla Ice Cream with
Fresh Strawberries

MEET ME AT GRANDMA'S
(serves 6)

Marinated Tomato Slices (page 43)
Country-Style Ribs (page 29)
Herb-Seasoned Green Beans (page 46)
Corn Pudding (page 47)
Cream Cheese Pound Cake (page 52)

KABOBS FOR FOUR
(serves 4)

Mixed Fresh Fruit Salad
Shish Kabobs Teriyaki (page 22)
Hot Cooked Yellow Rice
Minted Peas (page 47)
Cherry Cordial Dessert (page 51)

SUNDAY DINNER FAVORITES
(serves 6)

Simply Good Salad (page 43)
Marinated Pork Tenderloin (page 25)
Charcoal-Baked Potatoes (page 47)
Fresh Green Beans (page 46)
Easy Garlic Rolls (page 50)
Old-Fashioned Peach Cobbler (page 54)

A MENU MOSTLY GRILLED
(serves 4)

Tossed Green Salad
Honey-Glazed Chicken (page 36)
Vegetables in a Packet (page 49)
Grilled Garlic Bread (page 50)
Baked Custard (page 51)

CROWD-PLEASIN' COOKOUT
(serves 8)

Sour Cream Potato Salad (page 45)
Stuffed Hamburgers (page 12)
Barbecued Pinto Beans (page 46)
Crème de Menthe Brownies (page 53)

SUPPER PARTY FOR TEENS
(serves 12)

Country-Style Coleslaw (page 45)
Frankfurters with
Condiments (page 12)
Potato Chips
S'mores (page 53)

GRILLING FOR GUESTS THE FANCY WAY
(serves 10)

Lemon-Barbecued Turkey (page 32)
Hot Cooked Rice
Almond Asparagus (page 46)
Commercial Rolls
Deluxe Blueberry Cheesecake (page 51)

EASY MIDWEEK DINNER
(serves 6)

Tossed Green Salad
Grilled Grouper (page 14)
Easy Succotash (page 48)
Commercial Rolls
Cinnamon-Baked Apples (page 54)

SPRINGTIME FARE
(serves 4)

Spinach Salad (page 44)
Lamb Chops with
Béarnaise Sauce (page 20)
Parsley New Potatoes (page 47)
Summer Garden Medley (page 49)
Lemon Meringue Pie (page 54)

SOUTHWESTERN CAMPFIRE
(serves 12)

Crispy Coleslaw (page 44)
Grilled Brisket with
Panhandle Barbecue Sauce (page 7)
Fresh Lima Beans
Mexican Cornbread (page 49)
Cottonwood Carrot Cake (page 52)

SPECIAL FOR COMPANY
(serves 6)

Boston Tossed Salad (page 44)
Grilled Lobster Tails (page 18)
Zippy Zucchini Skillet (page 48)
Assorted Hard Rolls
Brandy-Chocolate Mousse (page 50)

Index